VOICES
FROM
THE
FUTURE

Other books by Children's Express

Listen to Us!

When I Was Young I Loved School: Dropping Out and Hanging In

VOICES
FROM
THE

FUTURE

Our Children
Tell Us About
Violence in America

By CHILDREN'S EXPRESS

Edited by Susan Goodwillie

Crown Publishers, Inc., New York

Children's Express acknowledges the Prudential Foundation for its generous support, without which this book would not have been possible.

Certain names and descriptions in this book have been changed to protect the privacy of others.

Published by Crown Publishers, Inc., 201 East 50th Street, New York, New York 10022. Member of the Crown Publishing Group.

Random House, Inc. New York, Toronto, London, Sydney, Auckland

CROWN is a trademark of Crown Publishers, Inc.

Manufactured in the United States of America

Photographs by Mary Ellen Mark

Design by Lenny Henderson

Library of Congress Cataloging-in-Publication Data
Voices from the future: our children tell us about violence in America / by
    Children's express; edited by Susan Goodwillie.
        1. Children and violence—United States—Case studies.
    I. Goodwillie, Susan.   II. Children's express.
    HQ784.V55V65   1993
    303.6'0973—dc20   93-20332
                                                                       CIP

ISBN 0-517-59494-3

10 9 8 7 6 5 4 3 2 1

First Edition

For William,
whose story has become part of my own.

CONTENTS

PREFACE

When I first began to tackle the astonishing raw material for this book—a mountain of transcripts of taped interviews of young people by young people across the country—I was stunned and shaken by the cruel reality of violence in America that their stories portrayed. It has become like a plague across the land, afflicting not just black children, not just poor children, but *all* children—black, white, Asian, Hispanic, rich, poor, urban, and rural. Everywhere, it seems, children are beset by violence—at home, at school, in their neighborhoods, among their peers, on TV, in the movies, wherever they go. Violence has become an everyday fact of life.

I was struck by the incidence of violence *at home,* by the number of parents who are disengaged, if not destroyed themselves, by drugs, alcohol, or abuse from their own parents. No wonder our youth are filled with rage and anger and unfulfilled dreams, alienated from their parents, from one another, from all of us. Their voices tell of horror beyond imagining.

And yet there is extraordinary hopefulness in their voices, too. Listen to Charleen and Christian, who are willing to forgive the most heinous and hurtful acts of violence against them, or to Darryl and Paul, who long for the opportunity to take *proper* care of children when they grow up.

Listen carefully to Tom Cat, Sonia, and José, who are trying to cope with their anger and hurt in ways other than by reciprocal violence; to Edwin, Pat, Quest, and Raoul, who have clear-eyed visions about helping people and being somebody; or to Leigh Ann and Twace, who have seen, and rue, the error of their ways. There are too many children in this book who have been victims of institutionalized violence in our society, but there are even more who have achieved excellence in spite of the incredible odds against them. There also, God bless them, is a rich vein of gutsy humor that gives these stories their ultimate life. These aren't bad kids. They are kids to whom bad things have been done, by their parents, by their institutions, by one another.

I think there is cause for hopefulness, if only we will *listen carefully,* not only to the young voices in this book, but to those all around us, to their cries for tenderness, for love, for simple recognition.

Please hear their hope—and see their vision for a brighter future. Many of them have not been welcomed generously into this world, but they still have an extraordinary desire to give of themselves, to help make the world a better place. Sometimes their dreams are realistic and sometimes they're not. But they all have dreams.

If you listen to the children in this book, you will hear a message from their hearts. You also will discover that we have, too often, abandoned them—as parents, as friends, as a society. If we don't reclaim them, we not only will lose our souls, we will lose our future as well.

S.G.
Washington, D.C.
November 3, 1992

INTRODUCTION

There is a growing literature today about the violent conditions that surround the lives of children in America. Psychologists and social scientists and many self-appointed experts have been flooding our newspapers, magazines, and bookstores with horrendous narratives and often pious explanations of the causes and the consequences of street violence and other aspects of the turbulent lives of young people.

Seldom, however, have our children been invited to express their own views on these matters. Even when an adult expert cites a child's words, the child is almost always used to reaffirm adult opinion. The context has been set by adults and the child is permitted only to provide a poignant bit of detail to relieve the dullness of adult discussion.

This patronizing tendency has had at least two obvious results. First, it tends to desiccate discussion. Adult views are, by and large, detached and dry; or, where there is any real emotion, it is generally a kind of protestation. Even worse, however, it has marginalized young people, denying them the central role that they deserve by reason of their own experiences.

Voices from the Future represents, in these respects, a powerful departure from tradition. Here at last we have an oral history of poverty and violence in the United States in which the questions have been posed and answers given by young people. It is a shocking and compelling work, refreshing in the vividness of detail, terrifying in the narratives that fill its pages, ultimately redemptive in the visionary longings that so many of these fascinating children and teenagers have been able to express.

There is, however, no false optimism. There are no maudlin resolutions of these tragedies. And many sections of the book—on gangs, racism, street life, and juvenile detention centers, for example—challenge readers with a sense of desperation that is almost unrelieved.

Nor do the children sanitize their statements in the manner that is commonly expected in most works by adult social scientists. Coarse and undisguised expressions of racism and homophobia are not rephrased or watered down by cautious editors.

I hope that adult readers will approach this book with undefended hearts. The writing is painful, as it ought to be. The wealthiest nation in the world has compromised its honor and betrayed its best traditions by an institutionalized, persistent, and sometimes sadistic viciousness toward its most vulnerable citizens—the only citizens who have no vote, no legal rights to speak of, and no public voice.

It does no good to tell a child that we plan to fix these things ten or twenty years from now. Ten years from now, these children won't be children. Twenty years from now, a shocking number of them will no longer be alive. The loss of childhood is irreversible. You never get to be a child twice. This is it. You have it once. And then it's gone forever. Almost any other theft can be made good by later restoration of the stolen object. But which of us can give back to a little girl in South Central Los Angeles or in the South Bronx of New York the years of childhood that have been stolen from her? The theft of childhood is irreversible. Time is the formidable enemy. This is why the stakes are so very high.

Perhaps the authors and the subjects of this book will have a chance at last to make their voices heard. Perhaps they will be asked to share their wisdom with the members of Congress and with our new President. If these things should come to pass, perhaps we may at last see a rebirth of wisdom—and of wise compassion—in our nation's policies toward children. It would be naive to think that we will see dramatic changes overnight, but we may see them sooner as a consequence of this disturbing work, and for this hope, no matter how uncertain, we can all be grateful.

—Jonathan Kozol

Car thieves, thirteen and seventeen.

Wake Up

Why in the world
Must we live
This way?

People are dying
Babies are crying
I've got something to say

It's time I spoke out
I'm really fed up with
All this

It seems whenever
We target a problem,
We always miss

People open your eyes
We've got to be strong
And willing

Let's come together as
One, love each other
And stop the killing

YOLANDA COLEMAN, 15

1

Violence,
Like Charity,
Begins at Home

CYCLES OF VIOLENCE IN THE FAMILY

*If my kids ask me about my childhood, I'll tell them it was
hard, but I made it.*

CONNIE, 12

Not everybody's life has to be this shitty, does it?

DIAMOND, 14

Girl with track-marked hands.

Death

Lightning flashes
Flesh is torn
People scream red rain falls

Sirens flare
tears fall making puddles
on the ground

The rain comes
on that dreary day
people put their memories away

RYAN FISCHER, 14

We went to Girls Incorporated to talk to girls who lived with violence but were trying to find an escape.

I took my group of four girls out into the bright sunshine, which seemed to contradict their stories of police cars and gangs roaming these same streets at night.

Connie was the oldest of the group but also the smallest. The sunlight made the fake gems on her shirt sparkle almost as much as her words. When we returned for more in-depth interviews, I decided to talk with her again because, unlike the other girls in the group, who wanted to watch cars go by or pull grass or eat powdered Kool-Aid, she wanted to talk.

When I entered the room, Connie ran up to me, hugged me, and begged me to be one of the select girls to be re-interviewed. As we talked in the basement, she never once sounded sad, even when talking about her uncle. Her focus was not violence, but her future and her dreams. Her enthusiasm for the program and enthusiasm for life gave me hope that she is going to make it.

Kate Schnippel, 16, Editor

CONNIE, 12, INDIANAPOLIS

I'm just a person that would try to stay out of trouble and do what is right, but I sure wish I could change all the violence and stuff that I be around and all the trouble that my family go through. Some of my uncles do a lot of drugs and the police is always after them.

I try to stop them from doing drugs and try to talk to them about it, but it makes me feel sad. I feel sad because they always told me not to do drugs. And when I see them doing drugs, it's like that's the person who told me don't do the drugs. They'll say, Drugs are bad, smoking is bad, drinking is bad, don't do it. Don't do this, don't do that.

I don't think I'll ever do it because the way it changes you and it makes you a badder person and really nobody would want to be around you. And your love for people changes. You start to hate people. Your whole personality changes.

4

All this violence around is terrible. When the violence starts to come, people start shooting each other, then the police come and they start beating up on people and everybody is fighting over something. Don't nobody really need that.

I got really scared watching the police come and take away my uncle, locking him up. He used to break into people's houses and get their nice jewelry and go sell it for drugs, for something he don't need. What made it scary is that I trusted him and he was always telling me, Don't go steal. Don't go do nothing. So I had it in my mind that I won't be going doing nothing like that, but then they came and took him away for something he done told me was all bad.

I felt scared because when I found out, it was like, No, that can't be him. They must've got somebody else, it can't be him, he's the good one. He's always telling us, Don't do this, don't do that. When I found it was really him, it kind of changed a little bit. Especially when you trusted him.

Kids learn about violence this way, either watching it on the streets, or watching through their family 'cause they're part of their loved ones. So it'll hurt them more if they see it in the family than if you see somebody out there in a gang doing it.

Violence and fighting—that's not it. It's not why God put us on this Earth. God put us on this Earth so that we could all know each other and be different colors, but He didn't put us on this Earth for violence. I think He put us on this Earth for us to love each other and give each other respect and stuff.

If my kids ask me about my childhood, I'll tell them it was hard, but I made it.

I interviewed Ruth at a place called Your House in San Mateo, California. She was there because she ran away. She lived with her grandparents but she did not get along with her grandmother.

Her father is a violent alcoholic. Her mother is not in the picture because she is a drug addict who lives elsewhere. Ruth is rebellious. She seemed very confused about who she is and how her life should be lived. She contradicts herself a lot, so at times it was hard to understand her. She was a little bit hard to talk to. I think she was intimidated by me. She seemed to be hiding something. Ruth needs a stable environment to surround her.

Sarah Young, 17, Editor

RUTH, 15, SAN MATEO, CALIFORNIA

My mom and dad got divorced when I was four, but my mom's a drug addict and my dad's an alcoholic, so my grandparents got custody of me. I lived up with them but I couldn't take my grandma 'cause I don't like her. I really hate her. She's the type of person who if you don't agree with her, she'll get revenge on you. And she won't even check it out to know the truth. So I went to live with my dad.

It was okay until he started drinking really bad again. He used to tell me that he had a lot of problems with my grandma 'cause she has a mental problem or something, and he showed me these scars on his face where she had tied him up and hit him with a belt buckle and stuff. So I think a lot has to do with how my grandparents brought my dad up.

But the one good thing is that I could talk to him about things that I can't talk about with my grandmother. And he understood that I had my own taste and that I am who I am. But when he drinks a lot, he would hit me. He's had a really hard life and I think he's just trying to forget about things. But I couldn't take it anymore, so I ran away.

Now I'm just waiting for things to check out so I can live with my friend's family, 'cause I can make it temporary custody and then permanent. I think it'll be a lot better for me, but it's really weird because they seem kind of phony to me. I'm not used to seeing family—they have family discussions and stuff. It's just something that I never had.

I have a brother but he stayed with my mom and I don't even know how old he is. I don't really consider him my brother because I've never been with him. I never really knew him. I just feel that I don't want to meet him 'cause then I won't know what I missed. I guess I'm kind of selfish, I don't know.

I guess now I gotta start thinking about my own future, what I'm gonna do with my life. Sometimes I want to be an interior decorator. Or I want to work in the music industry, 'cause all my friends, they're planning on getting in these heavy-metal bands. Some of my friends already got signed. My boyfriend, Larry, he's the drummer, he's in a band and I'd like to be in that. That would be cool. I guess I'd have to learn how to play something first.

Me and my boyfriend, we want to get engaged and stuff, but right now we're separated. We got in this fight, 'cause he wants to have kids, but I don't want to. And the first time we did it, I got pregnant and had a miscarriage. So I don't know with Larry. It's been off and on. We've been going out a month now, but we're separated right now 'cause I have a really bad temper and I get mad easily. So I'm supposed to talk to him today and see how things turn out.

I really like him, but it's complicated because my dad paid this guy to beat up Larry. I can't believe he did this. My dad was out front and Larry drove by in his friend's car and made some comment. My dad got mad, and he hired this guy to beat Larry up. But the guy was a friend of mine and so he got the fifty dollars and said he did it but he didn't. [*Laughs*] But now that we're broken up, like, the only reason he didn't is because that guy likes me. Since me and Larry are broken up, now he wants to beat Larry up. So I'm just like, *arrr*. I feel bad, though.

If my dad knew I was pregnant, he'd kill me and Larry. What got my dad was that Larry said, I was the first one to fuck your daughter. So my dad got really mad at that and made the comment to him that he would be the last one. Now my grand-parents even know. I was talking to my grandma and she's all, Well, I heard what your boyfriend did. I was like, Oh my God.

But you know, I wanted to have sex with Larry. Well, it wasn't till the last time we were going out that we finally did. We had been going out all that time, but I wanted to know that he really loved me. And he didn't mind.

I really hope me and Larry get back together because we really like to party together. What we usually do is we all trip a lot of acid. There's about ten people and we all kick back at someone's house all night. I like acid because you can use your imagination, like make your own world. And then with weed, it's just, you just laugh at the stupidest things. We always talk about things that happened before, you know, with all of us, how we all became friends.

So, right now, Larry and his friends are my only real family. And I mean, I have a very great family, because all of them have like police records and stuff. Yeah, they really care about me and look after me. They're my family.

I guess if I could change anything about my life it would be that my parents wouldn't be so messed up—just because they're messed up, it's coming down on me. I have to go through all this stuff, just because my parents are mess-ups.

I hang around with the same kind of people as my dad did when he was young, but I don't think I'm a mess-up. I mean, I'll do something with my life. My motto is, Live it up. If you die young, you die young. I'd rather have fun in my life than live a perfect life and live longer, you know? I like the excitement of the wild life.

Diamond and I had a hamburger at an outside table at McDonald's on a beautiful day. She was wearing a black T-shirt and black shorts. Her hair was a little above her shoulders, with bits of red in it. She was pale, kind of skinny, but very pretty, actually.

Talking with her was really heartbreaking. She had this distant look in her eye. I don't think she looked at me at all. She just sort of kept looking around. She didn't seem that eager to talk. She wasn't very open about her feelings. It was sort of hard.

Her father was a drunk and her mother just sent her to hospitals to find out what was wrong with her. She didn't want to go home because she didn't know what awful things might happen. She ended up out on the streets in San Francisco at fourteen, selling drugs and running errands for people.

To see a fourteen-year-old on the streets, with nowhere else to turn to—she really made me wonder what we are doing with the future of America. She seemed so resigned to her fate—that was one of the saddest parts about it. She didn't seem to have a lot of hopes and dreams and plans for the future.

Diamond seemed totally hopeless. She didn't see much she could do to change it: just got to live with it, survive somehow. I hope she'll find happiness out there.

Shane Tilston, 17, Editor

DIAMOND, 14, SAN FRANCISCO

I'm fourteen years old and I usually come down the street to hang out, just talk to friends. My home's not really functional and stuff, so I try to get away from it as much as possible.

My mom, she's like manic-depressive and she hasn't worked in three years, and my sister is really abusive. She's older, so she thinks she's the boss of everything and everybody, so I don't really like to be at home.

We're on Social Security disability insurance and stuff, so we don't get that much money. I usually come out here and try to make money somehow—you know, selling drugs and panhandling or doing errands for people—to try to bring home a few things at the end of the month. We're usually out of money and food, and most of our money goes for rent, so it's really hard.

My mom's very moody, she has rapid mood swings, and she's been in the hospital like eighteen times in the last three years, so me and my sister usually just stay at home and take care of ourselves.

I love my mom a lot, but sometimes it's really hard getting along with her when she goes through a manic cycle or depression. It's really tough to see your mom like that. I've had to take care of myself pretty much since I was nine, so mentally I'm kind of grown up and stuff. But I do love her a lot. She can be a really cool person to hang out with, but when she gets angry it will be like all of a sudden and it's just really hard to deal with.

Then, when she gets manic, she goes out a lot. Like me and my sister, we'd be about seven, eight, nine, and she'd stay out until two o'clock in the morning, and then we'd ask her where she was and she'd just start screaming at us, saying it was none of our business and we shouldn't worry about her. And when she goes through her depression cycle, she's just really depressed, she can't work, she'll just cry a lot, it's just really hard to deal with.

My father lives in Connecticut or somewhere, I don't know where he's staying at now. He's just a really bad alcoholic and he's a drug addict and stuff. I visited, but all the alcohol just totally deteriorated him and he was mostly very cruel and vicious all the time. He was troubled from his childhood also, you know. His father abused him and his mother died when he was real young and he really has a hard time trusting women. Every woman to him is just a bitch and they all done him wrong.

He'd get in a lot of fights with his wife—they are both alcoholics, blaming it on each other, so that was really hard to deal with. My dad would say stuff like, Oh, you're a bitch, and when they got in an argument with each other and I didn't take his side, he'd start saying I was going against him and that I wasn't his daughter anymore.

It's like, my father's pretty much abandoned me all throughout my life. When he finally did have the chance to be my dad, he was just this total asshole and chose the bottle over me. He just kind of took the easy way out and just didn't take the responsibility at all, you know, tried to avoid it and drink a lot.

It really makes me feel like shit, and I pretty much hate him for what he's done. I mean, it's his loss, that's how I look at it now. But I didn't at first. I felt like I was this bitch when I was living there. Then I went in the hospital because of what he'd done to me and then he started making me drink. So I've been drinking for about a year now.

I did drugs, too, to like escape my feelings and stuff, try to get out of it, 'cause I've been pretty much in a depression for the last three years, and I finally went in the hospital. But since everything is so chaotic at home, that just put me right back into it because of my sister and my mom.

My sister is very secretive about her feelings and about what she does. She thinks she's boss of everything. She always yells at me—you know, like if I don't put away something, I totally hear it from her, like she's my mom and stuff. I hate it, you know. She just, she won't leave me alone. She tells my mom everything that I do, you know, she's a real snitch.

I'm at the point where I can't stand her as a person, but I love her 'cause she's my sister. But, you know, none of my friends like her. She's, I'd say she's pretty close to, really weird. She can't get along with kids at her school at all. She was just like totally abused by kids when we were younger. I think that's probably where some of her problems come from. I mean, I really regret what they did to her, just 'cause, yeah, she was different, but they could've accepted her. Instead, they just had to tease her and totally make fun of her because she was different. I thought that was fucked up.

Now, I don't know what kind of future either of us will have. My mom's mother killed herself, 'cause she was this manic-depressive also, so it's like all over my family. My dad's depressive because of all the alcohol, and he's very weak and his liver's shot 'cause he's just a compulsive drinker, he cannot stop.

I know I'm an alcoholic and that comes from both sides of the family, but you know, hopefully when my mom gets back to work, I'll clean up my life, 'cause that's what I want.

I'm in school now. I didn't go to school a lot last year, but I made good grades and stuff, so they put me in a school right now that's going to let me catch up.

Then after that, I want to go to independent studies, which you only go to once a week and you do the work at home and stuff. I just can't imagine myself staying in the classroom all day long, you know, it's not me. I don't know, I just, I like to be free. I like to do what I want. I know I can't always, but I just don't like feeling that I have to do something that I really don't want to do 'cause I just don't like feeling like I'm in a cage and I'm all locked up.

When I grow up, I'm going to try to have a stable life, I'm going to make sure my life's back in order. I'm going to have a good, decent job that pays lots of money, 'cause I don't want to have to scrounge up what I can to eat stuff at the end of each month. I don't want to go through that anymore. I want to make good money and have a supportive husband. I don't want nobody like my dad who just runs out on every bit of responsibility.

Sometimes I just want to feel cared for, when I'm like in a real depressed state of mind. You know, sometimes I'll just feel good and I'll just be really happy and stuff. That's usually only when I take drugs. That's why I take them 'cause that's when I feel happy. Also, since my dad told me he'd rather have me smoke marijuana than cigarettes, I always got the idea that they were better and now I smoke both.

I wish that my mom wasn't the way she was and our family was better—that we had a father who would support us with work, that they both went to work and made good money. I wish I'd never got into drugs and alcohol, 'cause it really is a bad habit for me. I wish that everything would just be all right again, you know?

I guess basically I've pretty much been through hell on and off in my life. My life's just this roller coaster, it's going up and down with feelings. I know nobody can be perfect, but if I could just have something a little better than what my life is like right now, it would be so nice. Not everybody's life has to be this shitty, does it?

On his fifth birthday, Mark's father gave him a gun. At age sixteen, after years of being abused, Mark shot and killed his father with a rifle in their home. This is his story.

Suki Cheong, 14, Editor

MARK, HAVERHILL, MASSACHUSETTS

That was one of his things—we all had to learn how to shoot when we turned five years old. He made me go to karate and wrestling. My father was very big on fighting.

There was no time for anything except for my father. He always found something for us to do. You could go outside, rake the yard, be done with it, and then you'd have to go sweep the driveway, then go rake the yard again. You had no free time for yourself, no privacy at all. Every day he used to hit me, and one year he molested my sister. I found that out after I killed him.

I knew, even as I pulled the trigger, I was going to prison. I just didn't want my family to suffer anymore, or myself.

My father was hitting me one time and my mother screamed, Freddy, stop it. And so he started hitting her. And after he was done hitting her, he started hitting me again.

There was really nothing my mother could ever do. My mother was going to leave him one year when we were young and my father threatened to kill her mother if she tried to leave. And he would have done it, too. He was that type of person. There was just nowhere for us to go. My father was a very, very powerful man in the state.

I looked up to him a lot because he was a very, very smart man, very powerful, very influential. Kind of made me proud 'cause nobody would ever screw around with him. Everybody was afraid of the man. And nobody ever screwed around with me at all.

There was plenty of times when he'd throw my mother down the stairs, or beat the dog, and I'd want to kill him. You know, the thought would go through my head, but it wouldn't be something I was going to plan to do.

13

About two weeks before I killed him, my mother and I had a meeting with the juvenile officer in the police department. The police knew what type of person he was, but there was never any mention of child abuse from my neighbors, my teachers— even us. They told us they could put a restraining order on my father to keep him away from us. But we laughed at that because that man would have just killed us all that day.

It was December nineteenth, and I had skipped school, and the school had called my house. So I went home and opened up the door, and my father goes, You skipped school, didn't you? And he punched me three times and I fell to the ground.

So he beat me for about thirty-five or forty minutes, and he eventually picked up the hammer off the table and hit me in the head with it. After that, I crawled away and I went upstairs and grabbed the shotgun that was on my brother's side of the bedroom. And I walked by my mother and I said, Ma, I'm going to end this shit. I made the sign of the cross and I asked God to help me do the right thing and I shot him once.

It was weird. I don't want to say he trained us to kill, but in a way that's what he did.

The day I killed him, the cops arrested me. I was put into juvenile custody with the Youth Services. I pleaded not guilty. I was found guilty of murder because it wasn't self-defense or anything since he wasn't beating me at the moment I killed him.

They tried me as a juvenile, and when the eight months of the trial were up, I was seventeen and a half and they could only hold me until I was seventeen in Youth Services. So they gave me six months' probation. And I had to see a counselor for two years.

That helped me a lot. The counselor made me see things in a different way, like if I was to get into an argument with somebody, there was no talking anything out with me. You got a problem with me, then just fight me. Now, today, I'd rather talk it out than fight it out.

It's hard for me to get a job now because I have a felony against me. I got caught with drugs, too, a couple of years ago, so that's on my record, too.

I don't think it's right for any kid to take his parent's life, but under these circumstances, I guess you'd have to justify it. But I guess I just won't forgive myself for doing it. I really don't think I ever will. There's the torture that you have to go through when your parents are beating or abusing you. And then if you take their life, it's like the torture that you put yourself through afterwards.

It's your own flesh and blood that you destroyed. I have nightmares all the time. Your self-esteem goes. It's almost like after I killed him, I threw my own life away.

I believe he was raised the same way. My grandfather used to beat him as a kid. I remember him telling me stories about him getting hit with baseball bats and stuff. My father was an abused child.

Teens shooting heroin.

BREAKING THE CYCLE

Locking the kid in the closet for two hours, that's not discipline. That's terrorism.

CHRISTIAN, 21

I don't know that any kids today are really having these childhoods where it's carefree and the parents are there for them.

PAUL, 18

I was really sad when my father left. He was my affection. Out of all the things that happened to me, that hurted the most.

CHARLEEN, 17

We met Christian at the Pratt Institute in Brooklyn, where he was studying to be an architect. He was well dressed, clean shaven, and had a big smile on his face. He was black, a Haitian-American.

One of the things I remember about him was the sunglasses he wore. He said he had a problem looking in people's eyes because once when he stood and looked into his father's eyes, his father beat him for it. So he always had a problem looking at people. He said it had taken him a long time to be able to actually take off his sunglasses and start to look in people's eyes again. That was a really moving thing for me.

His smile is what I remember most. As we sat and listened to him talk, he got sort of sad, talking about his childhood. But afterwards, when he stopped, his smile came back and you saw that he had gotten past it, sort of won the battle against it. It was a true smile, one of those deep-from-inside kind of smiles. He's definitely a success story, I think, someone to admire for having gone through what he's gone through and come out the other side.

Shane Tilston, 17, Editor

CHRISTIAN, 21, BROOKLYN

I grew up with very, very strict parents. You know the deal, they did not believe in sparing the rod—in fact, they made bigger rods because they didn't think the standard one was good enough. [*Laughs*]

I got hit with extension cords, wire hangers, shoes, open hand—which was okay because they used to get tired and stop. The belt, I hated that fucking thing. My father used to use the belt-buckle part and my mother used the leather part, but she hit you longer, so you kind of had to flip a coin which one you really wanted to deal with.

What else? I got hit with walls, you know. You get grabbed and thrown against the wall, so it was like, What a lousy place for a wall. All of a sudden you go, *Bang*, okay, thank you. Or just picked up in the air and just dropped. [*Laughs*] You just pick up a little kid and, like, just drop him. Let gravity beat the shit out of him.

My father was okay, he just had a very mean temper. He told

you to do something and it had to be done. The problem was he would tell you to do something and my mother would tell you to do something else, and you had to choose which one you wanted to do first and you couldn't do them both at the same time, so you wound up getting in trouble anyway. I always wished that they would have a meeting or something and confer with each other on what the hell they wanted me to do.

My father was okay. I mean, some days he'd really be in a great mood, tell us to go outside and play—usually we had to be inside the house all the time—but it's when you messed up, you got in trouble.

I remember the time I really got scared was when he choked my sister. He had really huge hands and he put them over her face, and she couldn't breathe because his palms were over her nose and mouth, and she couldn't breathe and she kind of dropped to her knees and then her arms went limp and I figured she was dead. He let her go and she didn't move for a second. Then she took in all this air and I was like, Okay, good, she's not dead.

I wanted to help her then, but it would be worse if you tried to interfere. Like if I was getting hit and my sister tried to jump in, my sister would get hit and I would get hit worse for causing all these problems. So the best thing you could do for the other person was keep your mouth shut, make no noise, sit down someplace and do nothing, just do nothing to aggravate them. Then, later, you could talk to her, like bring her food or cold towels or try to help her afterwards. But you couldn't jump in. Jumping in was suicide.

My parents didn't really get along, but they supposedly stayed together for the kids. We wished they would split the hell up [laughs] 'cause we were like, Yeah, you're staying together for us but you're killing us, thank you.

My parents were very big on education. My mother was an A student since she was a kid, and she was also a nurse and an A student in nursing school. So, being an A student, she didn't understand B's, C's, D's. Anything under A was unacceptable. My father wasn't an A student, but he backed my mother and

19

let us know that coming home with C's and D's was not a good idea. An F, you were dead; a D, he wouldn't let you forget about it; and with C's, it would be like everyone would sit down at the table to eat and he'd tell you to take your plate and go inside. Get out of my face, I don't want to see you, get the fuck out of here. You just, you felt like dirt.

I was a B-average student, but there were times when I got C's and D's, which I paid for. There was never a time when it was like, This is great. Nah, you never got that. You got, Why can't it be A all the time? You never got a pat on the back, no.

I was always looking for my father's approval, and because of his violent streak, I guess I got into violence. He never called me by my name unless I was in trouble. He used to call me Hey stupid. Hey dummy. Come here. And I used to hate that.

I would sit there and be in a fight with somebody verbally and there's, Son of a bitch, your mother was a bastard, doo, doo, doo, and nothing, and then, You're so stupid, and *boom.* [*Laughs*] I couldn't take that and they couldn't understand why that would piss me off. They'd be like, All we said was you were stupid, and I'd crack them with a chair 'cause I couldn't do that when my father called me those names. I was always looking for my father's approval.

And then I got into weapons. I bought a little pocket knife one time and my mother found it and told my father and my father said, Your mother tells me you have a pocket knife. And I thought, Oh God, here we go. He said, Go get it and meet me in the garage. Yeah, he's going to stab me. [*Laughs*] I couldn't put it past him, I'm dead. So I go up to my room and I get it and come back down. I go in the garage and I'm scared and I'm giving him the knife and he looks at it. It was a rinky-dink little thing, and he goes into the glove compartment and pulls out a bigger one [*laughs*], and I figure we're going to have a knife fight, right? What is this going to be? And he gives it to me and he goes, Here, why don't you start a collection. He also went to Hoffritz with me to buy one of those Indian draw knives and stuff. So this was finally something I got his approval on.

Then my mom and dad got divorced and I guess during the divorce proceedings something went wrong because my father went home one time and crashed through one of the windows, took the entire window out—I mean, even the frame. He took the whole fucking window out, walked inside the house, and turned the alarm off. He trashed my mother's room, got out, made a phone call from the house, called my mother and said he's going after the kids first. He's going to kill them first and then he's going to bring the dead bodies to her and make her look at them right before he killed her. He was obviously very highly pissed off.

He never made it to my school. He decided to go after my mother first and it took five security guards to take him down. He spent the night in jail and that's the last I know of him or heard of him. He's gone.

So my mom had to do a lot of adjusting when my father left, figuring out that I wasn't just a robot to be ordered around. She had to learn that you talk to your kids, you don't bark at them, order them around, or curse them and then ask them for a favor. She'd be like, You miserable loser, you fucking bastard, come here and help me with this. [*Laughs*]

While my father was living in the house, he was like her enforcer—you know, If your mother says the sky is purple, the sky is purple, okay? And if I find out that you even thought the sky was blue, I'll break your fucking neck. It was like, your nerves were shot living with him because you never knew when the hell you were going to get hit. It was like walking in a mine field.

So, well, let's see. Where am I now? Well, after being extremely violent for a while—you know, taking all you can, giving as little as possible, never trusting anyone, that's the way I lived for a long time. I thought it was really cool.

And then I got into FACES,* where you had to trust people.

* Improvisational drama program for at-risk youth, sponsored by Miomonides Hospital in New York City.

You had to give in order to get, and there are a lot of rules about being nice to other people and not hurting people's feelings. Like, if someone got mad, my reaction was, Well, fuck you and get mad right back, you know, jump down their throat and then later on feel like, Damn, why did I do that?

And then I really got into this thing like I knew how to take things apart, I knew how to destroy things, I knew how to hurt things, but I didn't know how to create things. FACES has helped me a lot and I like my life a lot better now.

My mom and me even have a kind of understanding. She really wants me to talk to her now, 'cause for a long time I kept her in the dark. The less she knew, the less she could hurt me.

You know, when I start my family, I guess my child is going to mean a lot to me. A whole lot. I want to do everything with this kid, and I don't just mean the good stuff. I mean getting up, changing the diapers, getting up for feedings—I mean, I would live for that, to get up at two A.M. for the baby 'cause I want my baby, my kid, to know me more than his mind. It's like, especially if it's a son—oh, God, if it's a son—I'm going to go nuts. 'Cause it's going to be my son and I want to, I want to do things with my son. It will probably be the first time for both of us to go to a baseball game or a football game.

I just want him not to dread me coming home. *My dad's coming home. Oh, no.* I want to be able to understand that kids mess up. True, you gotta show some discipline, but you know, locking the kid in the closet for two hours, that's not discipline. That's fucking terrorism.

I met Charleen in a place where foster kids could go and hang out. We talked for a really long time. She was black and she had glasses and she was dressed nicely. She looked very grown up.

Charleen seemed like she accepted the things that were hard about her life. They were just facts and she was dealing with them. But she wasn't getting pity or she wasn't asking for any attention. She wasn't making herself out to be a sob story, or, you know, a really sad case. Her life just happened to be hard.

Charleen totally hadn't given up on herself. She's going to live for herself. She has goals and she has very definite plans for her future. Charleen really is motivated. She wants to go to college and be an international lawyer. I think she was looking at Boston University.

It doesn't matter that she can't afford to pay for college, she's going to get a scholarship. She's very intent on doing what she has planned. She's not going to let anything stop her. I think she does know that she's strong enough to do it.

She was this girl who'd just gone through five or six years in the foster-care system—being transferred from home to home—and she never had anyone that she could fall back on like her family. I'm from a middle-class, white background, but we could talk about lots of things that we had in common.

We've had different experiences. Obviously, I've had a much easier life than her, but I think that one of the reasons that we could talk so well and laugh and joke about things was because of our basic ideas. And I really respected her.

Cat Deakins, 15, Editor

CHARLEEN, 17, NEW YORK CITY

I grew up with my mother and my father and my three brothers. My father owned a business with my uncle. They were carpenters. They did everything, you know, build houses and everything. We were like a nice middle-class family, we lived in a nice place. I loved it, I had a beautiful childhood.

And then when I was eight, my mother, she started acting funny. She and my father were arguing a lot and fighting a lot and then she kicked him out and she told me that my father had lost his job. Well, I'm not stupid, you know. I mean, I'm like, How can you lose your job if you own the business? Anyway, she said he had spent up the rent money and so they had a big fight and she threw hot water on him. It was hard for me because I never really saw them fight and I couldn't believe it, so I grabbed a bat and I didn't know who to hit or what to do, so I gave it to my mother and my father pushed me and I fell into the wall and broke my rib. And then he realized what he had done, so they stopped fighting and they were all—Everyone was crying, especially me.

My father left and we didn't have any way of supporting ourselves, so we moved in with my aunt and my mother got on welfare. We lived with my aunt and her two sons and a daughter in a little tiny apartment. It was really crowded and everybody was grouchy and always arguing, so we used to always be in a corner crying, you know, me and my brothers.

And then we really couldn't take it, so we moved into this really sleazy hotel and my mother started going to church and met this church lady who told my mother that she was a sinner, and that's when the trouble really started and my mother started changing, she started beating us.

She started hitting us for no reason at all, especially me, 'cause she said that I looked like my father and I was the devil, like him. Sometimes I used to come in and she'd just find something to beat me for, really beat me bad because I was like really skinny, so it was easy to push me around. She used to pick me up and throw me. I always had bruises. She broke my arm, broke one of my legs. It was really bad.

And, you know, I got tired of that and I used to think what it would be like if I could get out of there. I used to see the Children's Aid Society songs on the television and I used to sing that and there was a number, right? I used to think about calling it. One day she beat me so bad that I looked in the telephone book and found the child-abuse number and copied it, and after my mother had beat me I went outside the house. She told me to go down to the church to clean the bathroom or something like that. Yeah, sure, I just got beaten, I can hardly move, and I'm gonna clean the bathroom. But I didn't say anything to her and she gave me the keys to the church. I went down there and I called the number and they asked me my name and all that stuff and told me to use my bus pass to go stay with my aunt for a few days.

So I did that and then a social worker came and took me and put me in an emergency home. I liked the emergency home. I still talk to her, my emergency home mother. She let me stay longer than you're supposed to because she liked me, too, and she wanted to adopt me, and I was like, No, I [don't] want to be adopted. But they were like, Yeah, you should be adopted. You know how hard it is for someone that old to get adopted. No one wants a big child, they want babies, but I didn't, I just didn't want to be adopted.

So then they moved me to my first foster home and oh, boy, that was something else. They were older people and they had a daughter they had adopted who was a year older than me and she was really mean and selfish, really mean. I had to do all the work and got blamed for everything while she played outside. I really didn't care for that and so I told my social worker and they found me another place, and that's where I've been for the last almost five years, and then I moved, just moved to the place where I'm living now.

I haven't talked to my mom for two, maybe three years. She couldn't believe what I did and used to call me bad names. She used to curse me out and I couldn't believe that, it was like, it wasn't my mother. That really hurted. And then they said she could visit me, but she only came maybe three or four times.

And then they said maybe I could go home, but when I went home for a visit, she tried to hit me, she slapped me, and then she told the agency she hit me and I was like, No, she didn't hit me. I don't know why. I guess she didn't want me to come home, she wanted to mess things up, and ever since then I was like so mad. I still don't understand how she could do that. She had my hopes up high and then, *boom*, that was it.

I miss my brothers a lot. About a year ago their social worker asked them did they want to have visits with me, 'cause I really wanted to see my brothers. My mother told them to say no because I was a bad influence on them and they didn't like me anymore. I knew my brothers would never say nothing like that. You know your brothers. Those are your brothers. You grew up with them, you know how they talk, what they're capable of saying and what they're not. We were really close, too. They listened to me more than they listened to my mother 'cause she was never there for them. I cooked, I cleaned for them, I washed them up, I washed their clothes. My mother wasn't around. So I knew they wouldn't say anything like that. But, you know, they're scared of her and whatever she says, they'll do it, not to get beaten or whatever.

You know, it's funny, my mother's the kind of person, I think if they took all her kids away, she'd just die. And, you know, I don't hate her or anything. I don't hate her. I used to say I hated her, after all the bad foster-home experiences, but then I think it's a sin to hate anyone. I got in touch with my feelings and, you know, I don't hate her, I can understand a little. She's my mother.

And I'm not scared that I will become like her. It's like that's my mother, I'm Charleen, two words, two different people. But I don't want kids, anyway—I don't even want a husband. [Laughs] No guy's going to be telling me what to do. I'm not cleaning up after nobody. That's how I feel. Since I want to be an international lawyer anyway, I'll be on the go.

My dad tried to keep in contact with us. It wasn't his fault that he couldn't. My mother wouldn't let him in. And when she moved, she wouldn't tell him where we lived. We each had to sneak and try to find my father and tell him, we told him where we lived and everything.

I was really sad when he left. He was my affection. I really loved my father. That hurted the most. Out of all the things that ever happened to me, that hurted the most. I mean, even one time, I was like almost raped, and my father leaving was more dramatic even than that.

Now I just love cultural things, learning about other cultures, other languages. I speak French real well. I wanted to go to France, but I went to Brazil instead. I got a full scholarship from American Field Service and I loved Brazil.

I guess I've been kind of lucky. I don't really believe in luck, though, I was just blessed that none of the really bad stuff happened to me.

I interviewed Darryl at Underground Atlanta. He looked like a typical black youth, any one of the thousands of kids you see around Atlanta. But his story was special and unique, and I guess that's sort of the point of this book, to give a story to the nameless faces that we pass on the streets every day. For some reason he picked us out or we picked him out.

One of the first things he said was that he came from a fairly affluent family. Both his parents were professionals, but that meant that they spent less time with him. That was the one thing that really frustrated him, that his parents didn't spend enough time with him.

Although Darryl had problems, he also had solutions. He talked a little about religion, a little about Islam and trying to find some sort of belief to carry him through. But he also had ideas for a school. He focused and knew the problems that he had with his own family and he wanted to change that in future generations.

Darryl was strikingly different from some of the other people we talked to who didn't really care about anyone else. They were so hurt with their own problems that they didn't really want to help others. But Darryl did. He also was very articulate. He seemed refined. This impressed me. He was one of the people we talked with that I think truly has the potential to make this world a little better.

Jess Scheer, 16, Editor

DARRYL, 16, ATLANTA

I guess my childhood was just what everybody would want. My father was a doctor and my mom's an insurance agent. As far as their economic growth, it's what everybody would want, but it was no family time. You know what I'm saying? Pop's trying to make the dollar so he can buy Mom a Benz, buy her snake-skin shoes and all that, but it was no family time. So you know I learned from my environment. I learned from the kids in the neighborhood.

Because there was no family time, I got whuppings for what I did wrong, but I didn't get rewards for what I did right. So it was always, Well, do something bad so at least they'll hit you, you know? At least you'll get some kind of attention.

I got an art scholarship in the seventh grade to go to university for a week during the summer, but my parents wouldn't let me go because of their own selfishness. They wanted to keep me as their baby, but they didn't want to raise me mentally. They just raised me materially.

So I started hanging with the bad crowd and I started doing bad things. Whenever I did get a chance to get out, I did a lot of stuff so I'd have something to remember while I'm locked up in the house.

And you know I did a lot of robbing. I stole cars. Had guns and all that whatnot. But every time I did something bad I felt funny on the inside.

I never used a gun on anybody, but I scared a lot of people with guns. There's a mind-set that causes the violence. If you have a negative mind-set without a gun, you're still going to hurt somebody.

And I don't think we can change people. We don't even know ourselves, so we can't change anybody else. I mean, I'm positive now, but there is still some negative in me that has to be destroyed. But I'm positive.

After a while when I was stealing and stuff, it felt so bad that I ended up stopping it and then I started studying religions. I was in Islam for a while and then that didn't satisfy my desire and I went to Christianity. But I can't change nobody. I can only give them information. It's up to people to change themselves.

I mean, the system is not helping any. As long as we are kids, we don't know shit. We're dumb and stupid and the system, they don't even let us vote until we're eighteen and then they don't give us no interest in politics. We be children, you know what I'm saying? We don't have no kind of interest in politics, but then we get eighteen, we all of a sudden got to vote and we don't know what the hell we're voting about. We just say, Oh, he looks good, he talks good trash on TV, let's vote for him. It's ridiculous.

What I want to do is start my own school. Ten years from

now I see myself in a class, but not a regular classroom. I mean, it's not going to be about surviving in this political and economic system because this politics is evil anyway. It's all about being better than somebody else.

My school is going to be a school of just equal teachers—you know, white, black, Hispanic, Chinese, whatever—'cause it's all about uplifting the heart and liberating the mind and body. Not the money game. Money can buy you the biggest Benz or the biggest house, but if your heart is not satisfied, you're still an upset person.

You don't earn richness regardless of how you look at it. You can go to school for all the degrees you want to, but you still gonna be a bum with degrees, you know what I'm saying? You don't earn richness, it's given to you. Richness is given to you. But it can also be taken away by your ties, your deeds, your works on this Earth. God don't claim people by their color, He judges heart. Judge every man by their heart.

Some people do good with broken homes. But when a child is raised up in a broken home, he got to find that outside support. If there's only one parent, that parent has to work hard to pay the bills. The parent has no time to just express their love, so he got to find love from somebody else.

I'm going to spend all my time with my kids. My job ain't more important than my kids, you know what I'm saying? I mean, they're not even my kids, they're just somebody that dropped here for me to take care of for a while. They're not even my kids. People say, This is my child, this is my child, but it ain't your child, it's God's child. I'm not even a child of my parents. I'm supposed to honor my mother and my father because their days have been longer than mine, but I'm God's child. I'm a son of the Creator. When people get their mind conscious and get out of this unconsciousness, they'll realize that.

As it is now, too many people let their emotions take over their mind. The mind is the biggest computer that man has. The mind built computers, so that means the mind on this

Earth is the greatest technology in the world. So if you can build something like that with your mind, your mind should be able to do anything other than destroy bodies. The mind and the spirit weren't put here to do negative stuff like that, to destroy like that. So I'd just ask them why, why they let their emotions take over their mental.

Then I would wish that universal knowledge would just reign on the Earth. I mean, universal knowledge—you can break that down in so many ways. Like positivity, you know, prevailing over negativity, intellect prevailing over darkness, you know what I'm saying? Just universal knowledge prevailing, just coming down all over the Earth. Because there's going to be a day when we all live at peace, even though we don't think about that now. There's going to be that day when people get themselves together and know who the Creator is.

We met Paul through Alateen in New York City. His story is really one of the saddest because there was a lot of physical abuse from his brother, which he couldn't do anything about, and some of the worse kind of abuse, which was neglect from his father, who wouldn't do anything about the beatings his brother gave him. He said he would cry in his room and no one would listen to him. It makes me so sad to think that all you had to do was go over and give him a hug and just talk to him, you know, just talking for a little while seemed to really mean a lot to him.

He had short black hair and was dressed pretty casually in shorts and a T-shirt. He seemed pretty relaxed about himself, the way he carried himself. He seemed to say, I finally found out who I am and it's good. But there was a sadness about him, too. Especially when he started talking about his parents.

He still has a lot of anger and resentment inside of him, even though he thinks he's getting rid of it. It's buried so deep within him, it's such a part of him, that it's going to take a lot to get him over it. As we were talking, I could just see him go back to the little boy, sitting on his bed in his room, just all by himself, crying, hoping someone would hear his tears. I wanted to just sort of sit around the bedroom and talk to him. Help him. Give him a hug. Because he's still got the little boy inside of him.

Shane Tilston, 17, Editor

PAUL, 18, NEW YORK CITY

I guess my story is a little different from most of the people you've talked to. I'm from a real upper-middle-class area. We were better off than most people, so a lot of things like unemployment and competing for jobs and stuff like that wasn't in our home. My dad worked his way out of all that and got us into at least where we were prolific in all the stuff we had.

But my mom was pretty violent. She'd spank us a lot and she'd scream and yell and they'd get into some pretty hairy fights. I remember when I was a little kid, it's like the only memories I have of them. Just screaming and throwing her

32

arms. The one memory I have of interacting with her was her whacking me, beating away at me and my brother.

They got divorced when I was six. She went away and my dad was against any kind of violence, so he never touched us. But my brother was pretty angry, I guess, and he used to get pretty brutal sometimes, so I got beat up a lot when I was little. It was a constant thing, like every day him beating up on me. That was kind of my role, I guess, I was just there to get beat up on. Because I didn't do anything else. I went to school and I didn't have very many friends. I'd come home and do my homework and get beat up and go to bed. My dad really wasn't in the picture because he was gone, he was at work all the time.

So my brother, he was like my idol, but he was weird. He was really brutal and he didn't like having me around much. I never got the idea that I was welcome near him. He wouldn't hang out with me or play games with me. But if it ever looked like he seriously hurt me, he'd make sure my arms weren't broken, that I was still breathing and stuff. I guess there was that instinct to take care of me, but he really didn't care too much about anything.

I think the divorce affected him a lot more than it affected me. He was older and he had a lot of trouble dealing with it—violent mood swings, and temper tantrums like crazy. Little things would just set him off and I'd catch it. I'd just sit there and get beat up. It was physical pain, it hurt all the time.

He was three years older, so he always had a big size advantage on me. Plus the fighting skills, so I had no choice but to submit to whatever he would do to me. I had no way of fighting back. And I remember a few times I'd just get in this rage, trying to do something to get back at him. And I couldn't, there was just no way.

When my brother got into the ninth grade, he started getting into drugs and drinking and that's when all the violence stopped happening around the house. He took whatever was going on when he was beating me up, stopped doing it to me, and started doing drugs and drinking, so it all went there. So I just went off on my own, too. And when I was fourteen, almost fifteen, he went into a hospital program and that's when I finally started talking to somebody.

For a lot of years, I had put it out of mind that he used to beat up on me every day. I didn't remember this until maybe three or six months ago and then it came out naturally, like, Wait a minute, I used to get beat up as a kid. I used to get hit every day. My brother would beat me up constantly and I had blocked it out.

See, my dad had this policy: If I told on my brother, he'd get sent to his room, say for two hours, but I'd get sent to my room for one hour, because my dad had to deal with the problem and he didn't want to deal with it. So it became more of a punishment to myself to say anything than to just not say anything. Just accept it. And I think that had a real big detrimental effect. It just closed me up and I didn't want to talk about it. If I was going to talk about it, I was going to get into trouble and I guess that gave me a message. It just set me down and down and down, to where I really closed up and I wouldn't associate with people very much.

You know, it's funny, I was director of a day camp last summer and those kids all seemed to be in the same situation. I don't know that any kids today are really having these childhoods where it's carefree and the parents are there for them. It's not that the parents are alcoholic like my dad ended up to be or in some far-off situation like my mom, it's just that they're working themselves like crazy and they don't pay attention to the kids that much. I don't think there are very many parents that really care so much that their kids are growing up and actually enjoying their childhoods.

I guess I just have to be glad for what I got out of it. Being strong and getting through any situation has its good and bad sides, but it's given me a lot of direction and I've been able to take a lot of leadership roles with it.

Still, there are emotions that have built up. There's a lot of loneliness. If I sit too long alone, then I'll start to get lonely and then a lot of these things will come back. It's not the loneliness of the night, it's the loneliness of all those years, the sadness. I never had parents, really. My mom was gone, my dad was at work or with his girlfriends, we had baby-sitters. My parents were obsolete. And a lot of pain—the physical pain of getting beat up.

The unanswered tears, you know, when you're just crying and you need someone to touch you and say it's all right. If I was crying, it was like, Get to your room. You'd run to your room and just cry for hours and hours and no one ever answered. It was like, What was I crying for? What does this do for me?

And then, for a long time, I didn't cry anymore at all. About nine or ten, I just cut off a lot of emotion. Not that I wasn't feeling it, but I just wouldn't let it come up, and I wouldn't recognize that I was hurt.

I wouldn't walk around depressed at all. I'd just walk around with nothing. From ten, eleven, twelve, until fourteen or fifteen, it was just emptiness until I got to Alateen, where I finally found something that opened up. I could talk to people and there was people who would listen to me and all those things that I had never gotten at home.

If I can cry, people come up to me and touch me, and those are things I missed out on. Not so much the childhood or the carefree playgrounds and stuff and laughing—although laughing is a hard one, too. It was just the learning how to grow up emotionally. I had no one to teach me how to do that. There wasn't a point in my life that was inspirational or heartwarming or anything like that.

Now I have to try and deal with the resentment and anger that I feel. There's a lot of it, more so for my brother. And a lot for my dad for not doing anything ever. I don't want to let myself get angry because I've seen what it can do to people—my brother's rage, how my mom would smack us and stuff. The sense that they were so out of control with themselves, that I don't like at all.

Resentment, yeah. But I know I've just kind of let go of that. The past is the past. I know also that my dad did the best job he could with us, at the time, because he didn't know any better. They say kids don't come with instruction manuals or anything.

As I look at it today, if he hadn't done everything he had done, and I hadn't gone through everything I had gone through, I wouldn't be this person. And today I do like myself, you know, good points and bad points. This is me and I just have to take it. Take me for what I am. Maybe I can help some other kids in trouble someday. That attitude is what's come out of the last five years in Alateen.

2

Innocent Victims

Sometimes I hear people that live upstairs talking about drugs. That makes me really scared. Most of the time I'm terrified.

JOSÉ, 10

I wish everybody would pay more attention to kids. That's something we really need.

RAOUL, 11

My mother stopped giving me the stuff to get high on, but by then I had other places to go.

JESSICA, 12

Children play "police arrest."

I sit and think,
Like a bird with its wings
Pinned beneath it:
Unable to fly.
Waiting for the tears to fall;
Not understanding why.
These people:
Afraid, ignorant.
Can they not see?
Why must I suffer?
What have I done wrong?

ROMY MANCINI, 16

I interviewed José down where the mailbox is at in the vestibule of my building in Brooklyn. It was about ten o'clock on a Saturday night and it was very noisy in the background. It was hard for me because at that time I was just starting to interview a lot of people. It was hard for me to relate to little kids 'cause all they'll say is yes or no.

José had curly, wavy, brown-black hair. He was nine or ten years old. He's Dominican. What was interesting about him was that he acted very mature for his age. He's not like all the other kids that were fooling around a lot. He's like a little man.

He talked to me about the drugs everywhere and how he feels about violence. He has opinions about that. He wanted to know why all this violence is happening. In that neighborhood, every day, all they see is people fighting with each other, people cursing in the streets, people taking crack, and they know it. They're not stupid. They know what's going on.

His father's dead, so now he's gotta be the man in the family. I think he's gonna be real handsome when he grows up. I love that kid. He may be hanging out in the street a lot, but I think he's gonna be okay. He didn't really have much fun when he was a real little kid, you know, not in that neighborhood.

Now he just has to keep on fighting, man. Losing your father and everything, you have to show your mother that you can do it. You're gonna want a big hug from your mother. You're gonna want her to say, "I'm real proud of you, remember that I'll be there for you, and I'll always teach you how to dance." I love you, kid.

Eric Zamora, 16, Editor

JOSÉ, 10, BROOKLYN

We live in an apartment. I like listening to music, and I'm scared whenever I go outside. Sometimes I hear people that live upstairs talking about drugs. That makes me really scared.

Most of the time I'm terrified. I would love to move out 'cause there's too much violence on this block. I used to get into a lot of fights, but I don't like to anymore. I used to be very active when I was a little kid, but now I'm just scared because my mother cries at night. I never told anybody.

I wish we could move away. I wish my father would come back. I wish we lived in a safe place. I just don't want no problems. I've been thinking about what might happen to me in the future and it's real scary.

My mother keeps me in the house now because people treat me bad outside. They used to take away mostly everything from me. I'd just mostly get mad and go upstairs. I wouldn't fight back if they were taller than me.

I know a group that wanted me to hang out with them, but they do bad stuff. They carry weapons, knives. I never really had a knife in my hand. I don't want to use one.

I don't know what to do because when the violence starts up, we're going to have to fight back. But I don't want to hurt anyone. Once I got beaten up in front of my friends. The kid made me bleed and everybody was laughing at me. Then I started crying and I got pissed off and so I kicked his butt. His name was Russell.

Sometimes I count on my friends. But I also count on myself. There's nobody else to protect me.

Raoul was a member of the San Jose Boys Club. It took us a while to get there, but we made it. I remember we went into this room and it was very hot. We told the kids what we were doing and they seemed sort of shy at first. No one really wanted to volunteer to be interviewed. But then when they saw their friends going to get interviewed, they'd want to get interviewed, too. My interviewing room was the kitchen. So we sat around the table in the kitchen, a whole bunch of kids, and we just talked. Raoul was the most interesting.

He is Cuban and he works with his mom and his stepfather. He lived with his mom and his first stepfather and then he got a new stepfather and this stepfather had a son. So they all live together in the same house and they seem to be getting along very well. He didn't seem to have anything horrible happen to him yet. That's good, 'cause he's only eleven.

He doesn't particularly like fighting, but he doesn't want to be a wimp either. His friends fight a lot, but he tries to stay out of getting into fistfights. He doesn't want to really be a part of that. He was just a little boy trying to live his life. I hope that he continues to believe that fighting isn't good.

Sarah Young, 17, Editor

RAOUL, 11, SAN JOSE

I live in San Jose. I like to play baseball and sports and stuff. I play second base, third base, and first base. I play a lot. I watch a lot of games on TV that I don't even like and then my mom yells at me to stop. She says I should read instead. I like action books because they get me excited. I like action movies, too.

I live with my mom. My dad moved to Miami when they broke up and I was about two. So I have a stepdad and a stepbrother. I'm not really close with my dad. I have a real close relationship with my mom. She's really nice and I love her.

My stepbrother and my mom get along, but not too good. He misses his mom. My stepdad took him because his mom was bad. And then my mom and his dad got married and we became a family. I think he would like to get his mom and dad back together 'cause he gets in trouble a lot. He lies and he manipulates people. He does that to his dad. He does little bed tricks, you know, I need water, I have to go to the bathroom. He takes advantage of his dad. He tries doing it with my mom, but it doesn't work.

Teachers say he gets in trouble at school. He's hyperactive. He eats a lot, but he's skinny. He's bare bones. He tries to break the family apart, but then we get back together.

My real dad's Cuban and my stepdad's Italian, so I know them both. I like Italian food better than Cuban food, although I'm not Italian. It's like I'm part Italian now that I'm growing up with Italian food and stuff. My mom's side is Spanish and Mexican. They're just regular people. No stars, no big managers or anything, just regular people.

I do good in school, but I don't want to do it. I want to get a good job and a good education and stuff, but I wish there was like a pill or something that you can take and it gets you out of school.

I try to stay away from fights at school. I don't like fighting. I just don't like getting hurt. When I was little, I used to get in trouble a lot. Used to fight. These two kids were my friends, but we used to get into arguments a lot. I beat them up really good. One of my friends was two years older than me. I beat him up. And I beat his little brother up. Then my cousin came out and then their big brother came out and that kind of settled things up. They started fighting and then the crowd just stopped the whole thing. I didn't really like it. I try to stay out of fights.

I try to settle things up by talking, though I will still get into a fight if I have to. I'm not going to just sit there. I don't like doing that kind of stuff, I only do it if I have to, if it's something big. My uncle likes me getting into fights. He says, Did you beat him up? My uncle's kind of crazy. He's Irish.

I'd like to design a building rather than fight. I'd like to be an architect or something like that. I've had a nice life so far, for eleven years, but I wish everybody would pay more attention to kids. That's something we really need. Sometimes grown-ups pay attention, but not a lot. They're kind of all wrapped up in their jobs and they don't really pay attention to little children. I think it wouldn't be so violent if people paid attention.

This kid named Roy was dark. He was black—at least, I think he was black. He was short and very smart. He's only ten years old, but he was very mature for his age. He takes everything easy. He avoids violence and that's what really got me to like him a lot.

He and I have something in common, you know—gunshots. He told me that from across his street in Atlanta they kept on firing guns outside. The same thing happened in my building.

He told me that he wanted to open his own program, like some institute where he could put people who were violent. I felt that he's going to have something going in the future. I'm really proud of him. He's the type that would never look for problems. Instead, he'll try to help out a person. I think that's cool.

Eric Zamora, 16, Editor
with Rolando Liriano, 16, Editor

ROY, 10, ATLANTA

Every night we hear gunshots. I don't know where they're coming from, but I'm used to it now. Usually, I'm asleep and I know it's nothing, 'cause it's all the way over there on the other side of the street. Lots of neighborhoods are dangerous. Mine is pretty in between. You see lots of fights. Anything can be happening on my street.

There are about two or three fights each week in my school, and about every day you see somebody up there in the office getting in trouble. One day I was walking home with my cousin and there was this big boy in a higher grade who used to pick on me every day. One day he pushed me and hit my head on a tree and I got real mad and I whipped his behind and he went home crying.

I'd like to start my own business, a sort of institute for people that are on the streets. I would try to bring these people to my institute during visiting hours so they could do what they please as long as they don't try to hurt anybody. It would be sort of like prison and hospital put together, but you don't get beat and you don't have people watching over you every two minutes. I would try to make it better for them and for other people. They would have somewhere they could unwind to, somebody who knows what they're going through. And they could just talk to each other.

I think it's important to have somebody to talk to because there's a lot of different people in the world and some people that look different might have the same kind of problem. Like if somebody come from all the way over there in New York City, if they come down here to Atlanta to live, somebody in Atlanta will probably have the same problem that they have and they could probably help each other solve it.

I try to stay out of violence. Like if there's a fight at school, sometimes I look at it, and then when the bell rings I just go home and try to forget about it.

If I had a lot of money, I'd get a clean-up pool that comes around at least two or three times a week to clean up the street and I would pay them for doing all the hard work. Most people does not like seeing all this garbage around the street, but they don't do anything about it.

If I had three wishes, my first wish is that there would be no drugs no more and that no one would throw paper on the ground. My second wish would be that my mom wouldn't have so much trouble getting stuff done for us and would have enough time to do her work and things that she really enjoys. For my third wish I wish I had all the best Nintendo tapes and someplace where I could be by myself. You need time with yourself, you know, 'cause you have to deal with your own self without bringing other people into it.

We worked on a series of roundtables about children in trouble. It was depressing hearing what these children had been through and knowing it's the kind of thing that happens daily.

I don't think you're born with a certain amount of charisma or intelligence. I think you become what you think you are. It's what you are exposed to in life that makes you.

Thelma Foster, 16
Jared Hoffman, 14
Editors

JESSICA, 12, NEW YORK CITY

Drugs were always around when I was growing up. I had no feelings about it then because me and my mother would get high together. I was used to it and I didn't think it was addicting. She would turn my friends on. I'd get high with her friends and then it just got to the point where I was getting high too often and my mother didn't know how to deal with it. That's when she stopped giving me the stuff to get high with, but by then I had other places to go.

I thought I could stop any time I wanted to. My mother was once heavy into drugs and had stopped. She just smoked then. When I got into downs and other drugs, she thought it got too serious and wouldn't turn me on. I figured if my mother could do it, there was nothing wrong with it. That was it.

When I used to get high, I used to get sick. I used to get very violent, and that's when I knew I was addicted. How did I feel? I *did* care for a little while. I was probably down on myself for letting myself go that far. But then I just didn't care anymore. At that time, drugs were more important—my main concern was getting high.

I find it hard to understand how anyone can come out of the setting that I've just visited without it having some real lasting effect on their lives, because the kids in there are incredibly angry. They all have a lot of pent-up anger and violence, and I don't see how they can leave here without having some mark of that anger left on them forever.

When we first came in, I particularly noted the locked buzzer door system. I can see why they feel the need for the locks because of all the boredom, the lack of anything to do—just the bleakness of the place.

Some of these kids are put in solitary confinement—total solitary confinement—for periods of up to three weeks. I mean, that's definitely the kind of thing that can really hurt someone for life. They are put in solitary for minor infractions such as fighting, which is totally promoted in the atmosphere in which they live, being confined together.

The playroom is empty except for a Ping-Pong table for which there are no balls, and there are just minimal toys, such as sponge blocks and wooden rocking things. I don't see how they can't have fights in this situation.

The kids we talked to are being represented by a lawyer as having been placed into this institution on less than fair grounds. They are kids who were essentially abandoned by their parents. I do not think that they belong in a mental institution.

Jared Hoffman, 14, Editor

PETER, 8

I was scared the first day I came here. There was a guy who was walkin' weird and I thought he was gonna come in our car. I didn't want to talk to him. I was so scared, I didn't know what to do.

And then I saw that lock on the door. And I saw the big gate and the wall so the psycho kids don't get out and the retard kids don't get in.

I cried in the time-out room a couple of times. Time-out

room got nothin' in it. It's a room and you can't get out. Collision room. They keep you in there a week or a day. Sometimes they lock the door and sometimes they don't. You pull the rug apart. Sometimes you climb up the wall and you break the sides. You put your hand in your pocket and go *bang, bang, bang.* Five days was the longest time I was ever in there. I'm eight.

RICHARD, 12

Time-out is better than meditation because you can lay down. I liked it because you can do a lot of things. You can hit the walls with your feet, but you have to take your shoes off because they're afraid you might strangle yourself with your shoelaces. Or you might kick the door down.

Walter was in twenty-one days. The deputy sheriff came, handcuffed him, threw him in that thing, and locked him up because they couldn't handle him. First time he came in here he came in an ambulance because his mom called the guys with the white coats. He wouldn't have come. There's nothing wrong with him.

We tried to escape, but I'm not used to running away. I was halfway over the fence, but then Harry, the guard, called me down. Anyway, the state pigs'll catch you.

JERRY, 13

One guy will hit you if you don't make your bed right. Barry's scared a lot and always makes his bed crooked. This guy comes in and picked Barry up like this with one arm and *smack, smack, smack.* Oh, they take care of us, all right.

George is the janitor and he wants to be a staff member. I bet he can be a staff member. You don't have to go to school to be here, you just have to go to a couple of staff meetings.

VICKI, 12

I wanna go home. I think about running away a lot. I cry in bed. I'm missing my friends—riding my bike, sleeping late, riding my skateboard, seeing my brother.

There's not that many things to do here. At least we can leave the unit for a little while, about half an hour out of the unit. We go up to the canteen and the candy machine. About half an hour to the Y to go swimming. We have swimming, kissing, staying up late. There's a lot of fighting because there are so many kids here.

The staff tells you to straighten up and try to get out of here. They think that they help. They tell you that they are helping, but they're not really. You help yourself.

On the streets at fourteen.

3

Coping Mechanisms: Fight, Flight, or Find a Friend

THE STREETS

You're just another person out on the streets. But I was safer out there than I was in my own home. At least I wasn't at home being beaten or molested by my uncle.

RED, 22

Sometimes when I'm on the streets, I feel like it's a total other society away from society, even though we have to live off society. It's like they don't know. They don't care.

KATIE, 17

I don't plan anything for tomorrow because I don't know if I'm going to make it through today.

PAT, 17

I walk along the gloomy streets
among maimed soldiers who deserved
something notable for their bravery.
Funeral pyres—empty reservoirs;
one frenzy ruined all of our lives.

DYLAN MORRIS, 12

We met Pete near Golden Gate Park on Haight Street. We drove down there and we were pretty much scared out of our wits. We got out and our knees were shaking and we went over and started talking to some people. I met Pete and we actually sat and talked in a bus stop. It was cold. He was wearing shorts and the side of his head was shaved.

Pete was different from a lot of the people we interviewed because instead of being very sad about what had happened to him, he actually came across as being happy with it. You almost felt sort of happy for him, because he seemed so happy, until you realized exactly what kind of life he was living, the kind of stuff he was doing. But his manner was very confident, almost to the point of being cocky.

He was very articulate, well spoken and open. He seemed well educated, said he came from a nice family. He had a lot of plans and ideas, and it seemed like he felt unstoppable, infallible sort of. It's hard to understand, but believe it or not, I could see that there could be an appealing side to that kind of life.

Shane Tilston, 17, Editor

PETE, 19, SAN FRANCISCO

PETE: I had a great childhood.

CE: Middle-class family?

PETE: Yeah. Upper middle class. My mom's really cool, both my parents used to be hippies. My dad used to be in a band. And they're pretty cool except now my dad's way conservative. And my mom's still, she's still like a friend, man.

But my dad's pretty antisocial. That's one of the reasons they got divorced. Because they didn't fight, they just didn't communicate. So, my mom doesn't make that much. She's still broke.

CE: What do you feel about your dad? Do you like him?

PETE: No. I don't think about him that often, actually, it's just not something I think about all that often. Once in a while I call him and tell him what's going on, that I'm a bike messenger or some bullshit like that. I tell him I have a place to live and I have a job. And it just keeps him from worrying.

CE: You tell your mom the truth?

PETE: Yeah. I tell my mom the truth. But she worries, so actually, I told her I'd got a job as a bike messenger, too, so she'd stop worrying, 'cause that's what moms do. Both of my parents know about all the drugs I do.

CE: What do they think about that?

PETE: My mom, she smokes pot once in a while. She thinks it's normal. Actually, both my parents, they know it's normal and they both have taken acid before and they both smoked a lot of pot, you know, drank a lot. My dad has a real drinking problem.

CE: So what do you do out here?

PETE: Sell things . . . whatever I get my hands on to.

CE: How much money do you get for that?

PETE: Depends on how busy it is, how much money I have to invest, you know.

CE: Roughly, on a good night.

PETE: A hundred dollars.

CE: And you use the stuff yourself.

PETE: I'm frying my brains out right now. Yeah, once in a while I trip. I smoke pot almost every day. It's easy to get free drugs. You need friends, but if you've got a lot of friends that are into the drug scene, you know, they want someone to party with. If you don't have any money, they'll pay for your drugs.

I've got a wide range of friends. Some have their own apartments, you know, you can go there. Right now I'm squatting with Andrea. I just met her tonight, actually, 'cause her sister bought some acid off me a couple of nights ago.

CE: Do you ever think that you're doing damage to the youth of America? Or do you just do it—

PETE: I don't think it's doing that much damage to the youth of America. Well, I don't see any problem with LSD and marijuana. There's a lot of other drugs, you know. I'm against cocaine, speed for the most part. I mean, I do it once in a while, but I've seen how that can like destroy people's lives. Alcohol. I hate alcohol. Booze is the worst. It's so pointless. You get really drunk and you do stupid things.

Hey, have you got a beer? [Laughs]

I don't know, tripping is a lot of fun. I guess if my first trip hadn't been fun, I wouldn't have been encouraged to try other drugs. I wouldn't have tried anything else. But I had a great time.

Have you ever taken acid?

CE: No.

PETE: Would you like to?

CE: No, not while I'm interviewing you.

PETE: Well, okay, I'll give you one to take home.

CE: My money's in the car.

PETE: Oh no, it's free. The first trip's always free. And it has nothing to do with being a pusher, you know—*Try this crap,* you know. It's not a big deal. I've had a lot of good drug experiences out here in California. I like to . . . especially speed . . . I like to do speed and then draw. I can spend six hours straight on one picture without stopping. I like painting on acid even better. Painting on acid, drawing on speed, and sculpture on pot, good stuff.

CE: So you're like a multi-medium artist.

PETE: Yeah.

CE: So what do you want to do in the future? Do you want to be an artist?

PETE: I'm not really sure. I really don't know. I think I should do something. Something constructive with my life. But it doesn't mean that I've got to join the middle class, you know, they're mindless boobs. Just something that I feel is constructive.

CE: Like what?

PETE: Bring down the government. I would say that was a constructive expenditure of my time. It's oppressive, the government, trying to bring down everybody else.

CE: What are they trying to bring down?

PETE: Well, parts of the lower class. The lower class. Poor people. And cops protect and serve the rich, not the poor, you know. I really don't know what I'm going to do with my life. Maybe I'll spend the rest of my life selling drugs and just have an easy life. It's not easy, but I won't pay any more taxes. Taxes suck. Why should I pay taxes? For what?

CE: For the lights in the streets and the school system.

PETE: Forget it. It doesn't cost them anything to make this. They have all their electricity for free. Why should we pay for it?

CE: Where are you staying tonight?

PETE: Hopefully, I'll be on my way to L.A. I have to go to L.A. tonight.

CE: You didn't mention that. What's that for?

PETE: Hell of it. I'm going for the hell of it. Some girls have business they need to do, so I'm just going along for the ride.

(At this point in the interview a man approached Pete, saying, "My name is Repo and I have to steal the car.")

PETE: He's telling you the truth. That's how we're getting to L.A. We have to get going.

CE: Do you mind doing this?

PETE: Nah, I don't mind this at all. No other way to go, man. Gotta borrow, borrow from a friend.

CE: So you're stealing a car.

PETE: No, I'm borrowing a car. We'll return it.

CE: You'll return it.

PETE: Yeah, in August.

CE: Really? That's great. Just slightly used.

PETE: Slightly used. No damage. We'll even probably re-gas it. A little bit.

CE: Is there anything you want to say to America about how you live, anything you want to tell the American public about you?

PETE: Yeah—you'll be hearing more from me in the future.

We showed up at the Youth Drop-in Center in San Antonio on a hot Saturday night in July. There weren't too many kids there because there was a big party somewhere else that night. There was a woman standing at the entrance, smelling people's breath when they came in. She was a big woman, big in stature as well as weight. She had greasy, long, dirty red hair that clung to her face. Her eyes were small, like pieces of black coal that poked out from her pudgy cheeks and stared at us through her thick glasses. She wore sneakers.

At first we were intimidated by her physical appearance and her street-smart attitude. She seemed reluctant to be interviewed by us. As she spilled out her story to us, we were amazed to see the callous expression on her face. It seemed as though it meant nothing to her. Little did we know that her story would bring tears to our eyes. By the end of the interview we understood her courage. What happened to her is ugly.

Amy Weisenbach, 15
Kathleen Hustad, 16
Editors

RED, 22, SAN ANTONIO

My real name is Monica Sheridan, but I go by my street name, which is Red. I was a runaway most of my life. I did drugs most of my life. I was molested by my uncle between the ages of four and eight. I was abused by my father. I ran away when I was eleven years old. Nobody messed with me after that.

I can't even remember how many times I ran away. I ran away a lot. There was times I slept out on the street. And I stayed from one friend's to another. I got in trouble. I sold drugs. I did drugs. But with all that I did, I wouldn't say I'd gone as far as other kids have gone. A lot of people got in it a lot worse than I did.

When you're on the streets, it's a feeling of being alone and no one to turn to. Nobody's gonna turn around and talk to you. Nobody cares about you. You're just another person out on the streets. I felt that I was free and I could go and come as I pleased. No matter where I went, nobody told me anything.

I can't really tell you how it felt out there, because I wasn't at home being beaten or molested by my uncle. I was out there where I wanted to be. I was safer out there than I was in my own home.

My mother would let her brother come and spend the night and I'd be in my room and I'd have to line up Coke bottles against the door so I could hear if the door opened at night. I'd leave the window open and the screen unlocked. That way if I heard any noise, if any of those Coke bottles hit the ground, I was out that window by the time the door had opened. I was more scared at home than I was here. The streets were my home. I was safe here and I belonged here.

Now I have a little girl, she's almost four months old. I spend all my mornings with my daughter. We stay home and we just sit there just like a mother and daughter. Then at five my mother takes her and leaves me off at work.

I figure a mother can be just as good as a father. He's not doing anything for us, anyway, so we don't need him. I can't support him and my daughter. So if he's not going to do anything for us, I don't want nothing to do with him.

I want my daughter to know what it was I did, how I lived my life. That way she'll know that it's out there. And I want her to know that she can come to me and talk to me any time she wants to. I think if you can't tell your mom anything about what happened to you when you were a child, then you don't have a relationship a mother and daughter should have. I want her to go to school. I want her to graduate. I want her to do something, to be somebody different. I don't want her to be what happened to me.

Being molested still has a big impact on me. It's like being cut with a razor and not feeling the pain until a long time afterwards. I don't trust anybody. It's made me rebellious and hard. My heart is hard. It's something else for my daughter, but for other people I mostly don't give a damn. Don't tell me anything. I don't want to hear it. It's made me hard.

I spent all my time fighting. But I'll tell you one thing: I've fought only one girl in my life and she beat the daylights out of me. I spent my whole time fighting guys, boys and guys and men.

My father used to hit me. My father and me, we never got along. For some reason he hated me and I hated him. I think it was because I reminded him of him. I was him. When he hit me, he hit me with his thick leather belt that had a big buckle that said Big Red on it and in the back it had a bottle opener. He used to hit me with that.

I remember when I was about seven, I got up to make my mom some breakfast. I was just putting food on the plate when my father came in and said, You're still eating? He punched me in the mouth and broke two of my teeth. Then he came back a few hours later and said, I bought you some cookies. But I couldn't eat the cookies because my teeth were missing and my gums were busted and my lips were busted, too.

I'm still working on my GED, but it's real hard. I'm not good at reading and writing. I got passed up all the way to the eleventh grade not knowing how to read or write. Then I quit. It didn't bother me until I got to the ninth. They just passed me over. Passed me as long as I got the hell out of school. But after a while it started bothering me that here I am, a certain age, and I barely learned how to spell my own last name.

This center, this place has helped me to learn how to read and write and spell. I'm not good at it, but I'm pretty good. I get up and read the newspaper. I'm kind of proud of that!

There's other kids here that know what it's like. They know that if you want to tell your problems to anybody, the best person to tell it to is a person who's been there. You just don't know what it's like unless you've been on this side of the tracks.

The kids here listen to me because they know that I don't take any of their crap. They know when I say do something, I mean do something. I don't tell them twice. I don't have to tell them twice and if I do, I'm just putting them out the door. I don't talk to myself and I don't talk to the walls. That's why they listen to me.

There's one girl that comes in here, she's a real don't-mess-with-me type of person. I realized every time she came in here that she got on my nerves. She got on my nerves real bad. Every time I saw her, I was like, I hate that girl. And then I realized she reminds me of me. No wonder I hate her.

Five years from now I want to have a good job, have my own house or apartment. I just want it to be me and my daughter. Hopefully, I can change my life around, maybe find someone that can accept me and my daughter. Start all over again. That's all.

When we went to the Larkin Street Youth Center, Pat volunteered to talk to us. He was about five feet ten inches and had blond hair. I don't think he had much schooling, but he was very intelligent.

The saddest part was that he seemed so resigned to his fate. He talked about what he wanted to be in the past tense, as if there could be no chance for him to change his life. There seemed to be no hope left in him.

He looked pretty healthy, but when he talked about the risk of getting AIDS, it was as if getting the disease would be better than his current situation, because then the state would take care of him. He seemed to be hoping to get the disease so there would be somebody responsible for looking after him.

Pat was pretty much abandoned by his parents and so he understood all too well that parents checking out like that causes a lot of problems. But I was struck that he was so thoughtful about it. He wasn't angry. I feel very sad for him.

Shane Tilston, 17, Editor

PAT, 17, SAN FRANCISCO

My mom's a heroin addict. She's been an addict since thirteen. She went to a party when she was about sixteen, got drunk, got screwed, and that's how I got here. I wasn't exactly planned, you might say. From when I was born until I was three, she couldn't take care of me. I stayed with my grandfather a lot. We used to sleep in the car.

Then, when I was three, the state took me in. Started tossing me around to different foster homes and stuff. I went to about twenty different foster homes, and by the time I was seven I had finally gotten adopted. After that, I had life set up the way I was going to run it. Nobody else would take care of me, so I'd take care of me.

Nobody else was there for me. If I got hungry, I went up and fed my face. I wasn't afraid of being a street urchin or whatever a person might consider me as. I had no choice and I had to make do with what I had.

When I was six, I ran away from the adoption home because

I got molested. My foster father did it and said, If you tell anybody, I'm going to kill you. At first I thought about it and I was like, Whoa, he would kill me. But then I thought some more and said, No, he can't kill me because he already did it. So I started trying to tell people, but nobody would listen to me. They wouldn't believe me. I felt like I was a disease.

I was on the streets for about six months before they finally caught me. They took me back and I got adopted about a month after that. My adoptive mom was really sick, so my dad didn't mess with me too much. I knew from the start that he really didn't like me and it wasn't fun. He tolerated me until my mom died and then we started getting into fights.

When I was about fourteen, he hit me one time and I blacked out. I had a scar across my ribs. Finally, I said, Fuck it, I just can't take it. So I took off. He typed up some papers and had them legalized and I had his permission to be on my own. You know, make sure that I couldn't come back.

So I've just been traveling around. When I first got on the road, I was hitchhiking and a guy picked me up and offered me some money for sexual favors. It was like a way to survive and all I had on my mind at the time was survival. Even now, I hustle the streets to survive. That's where my income comes from. I have nothing else. Not a high-school equivalent, nothing.

I don't particularly like to do it, but I have no choice. I have to squat at night unless somebody picks me up and gives me a place to stay for the night. It's really rough being on the streets. If I did have a chance to get back to a home and school and all that, I probably wouldn't be able to fit in because I've been on the streets for so long and I'm in a survival mode, I'm not in the family mode. I guess I've been in a survival mode all my life. I never knew anything else except the survival mode.

When I got on the road, I started spooning some different drugs. I started to smoke a lot of pot, dropping acid and speed, started smoking heroin, even got into opium. It's like steadily killing myself. I just quit it all now, except for some pot whenever somebody offers it to me. I don't buy it. It's just too dangerous.

Hustling is dangerous, too. It's like playing Russian roulette. I gotta do what the person wants. If he wants me to wear a condom, I'll wear a condom. If he doesn't, then there's nothing I can say about it. It's like, Well, I can say no and be out of money for that night. And then he tells all his friends and it ruins my business.

If I get a disease, I'm going to commit suicide, and if I don't, then I'm going to keep going. It's like it really doesn't matter to me, because it can't get much worse except for death. Only thing it can get is better, so either way it goes, something's going to happen.

If I contract the AIDS virus, at least I'll be able to live nice without having to live on the streets until I die. When you're HIV-positive, they pay for everything, you know. It's like no problem. They give you food stamps, they have meals and stuff every day that's delivered to your house.

I just watched a lot of my friends getting hurt and I know exactly what's going to happen to me if I do get it, so I'm not afraid of it. When you've been out in the rain, you really don't give a shit about anything, you know. You don't care whether you live or die. Each day, I don't plan anything for tomorrow. I don't plan anything for tomorrow because I don't know if I'm going to make it through today.

I'm out there every night, and during the day I hang out at a shelter for a little while and then I go out and panhandle so I can have some money for my friends to eat. I take care of my friends that are out there because they have nothing. They try to survive on panhandling, but it's tough. I buy them food or whatever they need. It's like they're my family. They're the only family that I know and I want to take care of my family. They take care of me whenever I need it and they have something. So I take care of them. I take care of all my friends. It's just the way I figure it should be.

I've always helped my friends out. They call me their problem solver. Everything that they're going through now, I've already been through and dealt with it and solved it, so they come to me. When they got a problem, they ask me, How do I solve it? And I tell them the way I solved it.

Take anger, for instance. I've pretty much figured out how to deal with my anger about nobody wanting me, you know, but it was hard. I'd tried my hardest to be exactly what they wanted me to be. Or I'd try to be myself. Whatever. And they'd just keep me for a month or two and then toss me away. I went to at least fifteen different schools and it was not really cool.

I can get rid of the anger, but anger is a feeling that everybody has and they'll have to deal with it until they die. People say anger is like really bad. No, anger's not bad, it's how you deal with it whether it gets bad or not. I deal with it in a positive way. I try not to do violent stuff.

I keep in touch with my mom every once in a while. I call her up and say, Well, I'm alive, good-bye. I don't want to hear what she has to say. She could take me in. She could give me a home and all if she wanted to. But she doesn't. I'm out here on the streets and what does she do? She walks right on by. I suppose I love her because without her I wouldn't be here in this world. But I hate her because she's making my stay in this world hell.

I used to think street gangs gave me the best protection. I was like really running scared. I didn't have anybody to turn to. Didn't know anything about the streets. So violence was a way of having protection. I felt safe is what I thought, at least.

But I don't believe in the violence shit anymore. I mean I try to avoid certain things if I possibly can. When I'm out on the streets, it's a different story. When I'm working, that's a different story. I have to be violent when somebody's violent with me. Because it's either them or me. But when I'm in the shelter and somebody's played up at me and wants to fight, I'll solve it without fighting.

I have always been real good with words. It's psychology. I wanted to be a psychologist, you know. I wanted to be a medical doctor and work at a free health clinic to help people out and get paid for that.

I see these people out on the streets and they have nothing. There are these doctors around in America and the only thing they're worried about is getting their paycheck, getting as much money out of you as possible. I mean you can't even get into a hospital unless you got a thousand dollars right there at the desk. That's just for the room. Getting medical attention, you've got to have like six thousand dollars. And what can you do when you need to find out what's wrong with you?

But that's just not me, you know. I'd get paid for helping people with mental problems, emotional problems, and stuff like that, but not for medical problems. And if you know that they're dying, I'm going to help them out for free. If they're like having a problem with their dads, I'll let their dad pay for it.

If we're going to deal with violence, people need to sit down for a minute and take a look at their kids, see how their kids are living, and then take a look at what's going on in the world. Go downtown wherever you live and take a look at it. Look at the homeless people there. There's kids in every town that are homeless and they're out on the streets. And if you want to understand, then go out there and just sit down and talk with one of them.

Parents need to be a little less ignorant about what their children do. They need to be more open to it. Instead of looking at it in a black-and-white picture, they need to look at it in color. When parents treat their kids like they have a brain and try being friends with them, or try to become some-one on an equal level, then you can get a lot of their problems solved.

Nine out of ten kids that are out on the streets now are out here because their parents kicked them out or they were run-aways because their parents didn't understand them. They wouldn't sit and talk with them. My dad wouldn't talk with me. He beat my ass.

We met Katie and Kelly outside the Larkin Street Youth Center in San Francisco. They are sisters and they were very, very punk. They wore black, all black. Kelly had bright red hair and tattoos. Katie had long black hair and a tattoo on her forearm all the way down to her hand. Very heavy-metal looking.

They were both young, and they've been out on the streets for a long time. They stay in shelters sometimes to get free meals. And they talked about survival sex that they do, just to make some money to stay alive.

Their life seems really unfair, but it was interesting because they had each other. They always relied on each other and had each other to talk to about what was going on. That also helped them with their plans for the future. They plan to get a house together and I think they kept each other going.

They were really strong people mentally. It's amazing the stuff they had gone through and the way they stuck together and helped each other out. They just have this incredible loyalty and bond. I really admire that.

Shane Tilston, 17, Editor

KATIE, 17, AND KELLY, 15, SAN FRANCISCO

KATIE: I'm Katie and I'm seventeen years old. I'm growing up and I'm using lipsticks. Kelly is fifteen and we're sisters. We don't have parents because we're in the system. Our parents destroyed, abused us. They got arrested and we got taken away. We have a little brother and a little sister, but we don't know where they are.

We've run away from a lot of system places. We live on the streets out of necessity. There are a lot of people like us. There are some that can't go home 'cause they were kicked out. And there are some that just need the time.

I don't like it, really. At first it was like massive freedom. But now I just got released from the system, after eight months on the run, and I know I can do better. It's boring for me now, because it's not freedom anymore.

We don't have the freedom to go out and have fun with our

friends, which we would be able to have if we could live like normal people, in a house. We have to go out and spend our time looking for food, doing this or that to survive. It is better than being home, but it's not a party. Not at all. I feel like I've done most everything there is. I want off, but it's hard to get off, it's like a cycle.

We're still on a squat, but we're on the waiting list to get into Hospitality House. We had an interview today, but we didn't make it because in our squat everyone's so loud and they get drunk all night and they were all up in our room until three o'clock this morning. So we didn't wake. We're about to go over there now and tell them, you know, we're sorry, but we couldn't make it this morning.

If we get in, I'd like to do something in the arts. I did my high-school diploma while I was on the streets. I did an independent study. I was like sneaking to the library to do work and living off friends, and so I graduated and I want to go to college. I want to learn journalism, or maybe law.

After all the stuff that has been negative that we had to go through in the system, I want to try and do something positive. I want to write a book. I had all these journals that they kept taking away from me. I still have some writings, though. I write a lot. I write a lot of poetry, stories, and journal entries. I like music, too. As a kid, I was always into that. I want to get back into that because I really loved that.

KELLY: I want to get my GED. I've got three more years left of school. Fuck that, it's too long. I want to do something creative. And when I get enough money, I'm going to go around and help street kids, because I know what it's like out here. Sometimes they do buy booze and everything, but they also need food. I'd like to help them out as much as I can. I'm not going to bring them into my house, because they'll steal everything. But I'll try and do my best. I want to become a psychiatrist because I hate shrinks. I totally hate shrinks, but I would be different.

KATIE: Me and my sister got separated because about two years ago we went into a mental institution. They told the doctor that we had a suicide pact, so they separated us. We got separated for about eight months and then we saw each other for a while and then, when we were on the run, they threw us in a home and my sister escaped after about three days and we got separated again for about two years. We didn't know where each other was at all, until just now when we got reunited. It's a long story how we found each other, and we were so happy to see each other after two years.

So now we're back on the streets and there's all sorts of different ways to make money. Panhandling is the biggest thing, but that doesn't usually get all our money. Sometimes we rob places—stealing food, that's always a big thing. We used to go to doughnut places and like snitch doughnuts and run out and someone would wait around the corner. Then when they're all chasing you, you go on back and hit the cash register and take all the money.

KELLY: I also got clothes by mugging people in Hollywood. We used to mug druggies. We used to tell 'em, Oh, yeah, we know where you can get a really good deal here, and then you go and jump them and take their money. It's not that bad 'cause they're like scum anyway.

You know, they're all street people like us. And that's how they make money. They're doing terrible things to make money. They victimize themselves, each other.

I've sold drugs before but I never prostituted. I've gone through the thing where it's easier to just sleep with someone that I meet, though. I hate the idea of having to sleep with some fifty-year-old perverted man, but sometimes I really need a place to stay and I don't have anything else better to do. And he needs someone. And you fuck them and you know as long as you're fucking them you can stay at their house.

I kind of like my friends on the streets. It's not like a close thing, it's not like a family like people think, it's really kind of lonely. But here you have your friends, and you make really close friends by need or necessity. I've had them support me. I've had really good prostitute friends who'll get the hotels and we'd all stay there and contribute.

Like in the squats, you have to contribute, too. We only let people in if they have drugs or food. I can steal food pretty good. I haven't been caught lately at all. Well, I've been caught, but I've never been pulled in. It all depends on how daring you're willing to be. You know, me and this other girl were living in the squat and we used to go and steal things, but we would never get pulled in because if someone tried to stop us we'd just punch their lights out.

KATIE: She beat up the manager at 7-Eleven. She's pretty violent if it's out of necessity, or when she's mad enough.

KELLY: Inside of me I don't think that I'm really a violent person. I think that kids on the streets are basically good, but it's just that they do it out of necessity. And sometimes they become violent because they're blinded. They get corrupted or twisted because of what they have to do.

I've had friends turn into prostitutes and they were totally cool and innocent beforehand. Afterwards, they get to where they have to trick themselves into enjoying sex, you know, with gross old men who have really kinky ideas. They used to tell me stuff that wasn't pretty at all.

After a while it changes you and it blinds you. You learn how much violence you can get away with and you learn how to get away with it.

The only thing I've ever done was panhandle. I can sit there for days, but when San Francisco gets really cold and the people are like, Fuck you, it really gets me so mad. I'm not a mean person, I just get mad when people tell me to fuck off when I'm sitting out there starving to death. They tell me to go home, or get a job. I don't have a home and I'm fifteen years old. It's really hard to get a job, but I'm going to try and get a job. That's one of my main goals—and an apartment. Then I'll be happy.

73

KATIE: I don't care what I do, I'll do whatever to get off the streets. But times are hard, you know, I've called real jobs before and, you know, you've got no money, you're on the streets, you're staying in the squat, you have to wake up in the morning, which is hell because everyone's running through your room drunk.

Even if you get a job, you don't get your first paycheck for about two weeks, so you have to starve till then. I had a job, only a few months ago, and at every break I had to go out and steal food at the places nearby because I had no money at all. I didn't have any clothes, either. It was hard. It was really hard to start.

KELLY: At shelters, they're really stupid because they say you have to have parental consent. If you don't have parents, you have to lie, and then they get suspicious and ask more questions, and so you have to lie some more. It's really stupid.

KATIE: Another thing on the streets a lot is rapes. I don't have them as much, because I'm more smarter, but back when I was fifteen, I was getting raped at least once a month. Each time I would try to learn something, but still, you can't really trust your friends on the streets.

One time I got raped by this pimp. I needed medical care for it. And that was like really bad because actually he beat me up and then he raped me. And you can't report it when you're on the run. You feel real bad about it because you can't do anything about it. If you call the police, you get pulled in. Why make your life worse? When I needed medical care, I used different names and stuff and I got help. I was fifteen and they couldn't use my insurance or anything, so I ended up paying like hundreds and hundreds of dollars and then I had to leave the hospital before they found out who I was.

The system is really horrible. It's like they don't care about you at all. They just get more money when you stay there. They don't really look into your case and stuff. When they put you in, you feel like a guinea pig. One time I broke into my files and they all had these massive charts, just like an experiment. They treat you like an animal in an experiment. It's all bullshit. I totally hate it.

KELLY: You forget who you are when you're in an institution. They treat you like shit. They do everything secretively, like when they move you, or when they are taking you out of your place so your friends won't know.

I was in this group home and I really liked it, and they told me that I was going to be moved to a detention home for three days and I was coming right back if I was good. I was depressed because my sister was gone, but I had a best friend who was with me, we were roommates, so they moved her out because they thought I was going to run away with her. They kept lying to me and telling me, Oh, her grandmother is sick and she'll be back in a week. And, Oh, it had to be extended, she'll be back next week. Then they came and packed up all her stuff and I was so depressed.

They never planned for me to come back, they replaced me the next day. They gave all my stuff to all the girls. And here I am at this detention home, trying to be good, and they left me there. Then I found out that they planned to put me in an even worse place after that, a bigger detention home. They just constantly lied, all the time. They always tell you that you're going to a better place, but you're really going to a worse place. It's just massive bullshit.

Then they put you in a juvenile home someplace, where it's supposed to make you better. But you're with all these other kids that are totally unstable and going off because they think it's fun. They think crimes are fun. I mean, that's where you get your crime partner. The whole system is bullshit. They don't even give you a chance. You don't even feel like a real human being.

One of the worst things they do is strap you. You're only supposed to be strapped for like six hours at the most, but I've been strapped for two days in a row. They shoot you up with drugs when you're strapped and they use the same needle for everybody. I hate being strapped. I hate it.

It's all these little things, they all add up. They drug you over and they don't tell you what drugs. They just all of a sudden come in the morning, after your last psychiatrist session, saying they have this new little pill. And you say, What is it? And they say, Take it, take it. They drug you up so bad you can't even get up and go to the bathroom or see straight. You're drooling and stuff, because it calms you down. It's like easier for them if you're sitting on your bed drooling and you can't even get up or see straight. That's what they like to do.

KATIE: They don't let you keep journals, they don't let you write about what's going on. You have no contact with the outside world. You don't even know if there *is* any outside world. It's like a nightmare from hell.

They rob you of everything. For me, the most important things are my writings. I want to reach out to people through my writing. I want to let people know. But they took them away and they never gave them back to me. They lose all of your stuff. It's the first thing they do, the staff and social workers, they take your stuff. And you never get it back. You never do.

I don't know any kids who've had a good experience with the system at all. It is not a growing experience. I want to do something about it, but right now I know I can't. I need to get my own life together.

Sometimes I wonder why I had to go through it, and sometimes I wonder if it was a test for me. Sometimes I feel that it might have been part of what I'm supposed to deal with when I get older. Maybe when I get older, I'll explore everything and tear it big wide open. I don't know, I wonder if there's a real purpose for it. I think that everything you go through must have a purpose for it. Even if it's not, it can turn into a learning experience. But sometimes I really feel victimized by it.

KELLY: You know, the system for me was such a nightmare, I constantly wanted to die. But I won't, because I swore I was going to make it through and stick my middle finger in their face. I was going to see my sister again. Now I see my sister and I want to live with her and I want to live for her. I want to get my life to where it's something great, where I can like it a lot.

If we've gone this far, we can go a lot further. I can see now that there has to be a way out of it. I keep trying now and I know I'm eventually going to do it.

What can you do when you've got someone that's out for you because you ran away from someplace that was hell? Even for kids in our cases, like their parents don't want them anymore, or they kick them out because they're obnoxious, or they beat them, or whatever the condition. I think there will always be kids on the street.

I want something to be done about it. I want people to know what's going on. Because there are some times when I'm on the streets, I feel like it's a total other society away from society, even though we have to live off society. It's like they don't know. They don't care.

People need to find out that it's not easy and a lot of kids out there really don't have chances. A lot of people think in America everybody lives with their parents, they have a really nice time, go to college, get a job, and live in a house with a white picket fence. But that's not the way it is for everybody. There are so many kids out there where it isn't like that and they simply don't have a chance. I think people should actually be willing to give them a chance, at least for the kids that really want to do good.

I've felt like people are scared of me on the streets. Especially when they know you're homeless and they think you're a criminal or something. They're walking by and they grab their kids and stuff 'cause they think you're going to mug them or something.

KATIE: A lot of people plan to die in the street. They talk about how they're going to die from overdose and what a cool way to die, before they're even twenty years old. A lot of them really plan to die. A lot of them have given up on life.

77

You can only have hope for just so long and then it just dies out. We still have hope. We'd better have hope! We're gonna get off the streets, dammit.

The injustice in this society is that there will always be kids on the street. I think the more there are, the more the kids will be on the street because there's nothing else to do. There's nothing else for a lot of them. They can't get jobs and apartments.

Then there are people who are walking by in their minks and getting out of their Mercedes cars. They don't see much. They don't know much of anything. And they don't care. The majority of them out there don't care. They're just locked up in their own little world.

I'd say to kids, If you have a nice home, don't fuckin' come out on the streets, man. Just go home, all of you, turn around. If you have a nice VCR and TV and nice parents, don't come out here. It's not parties. It's not a wonderful time. You're not free. Freedom is a foreign partner out here.

People are only worried about what's going on with their own little world. But just imagine—we're the next generation that's going to be *running* the world. And if we're all fucked up, you're going to have a really fucked-up world.

School

School was my church, it was my religion. It was constant, the only thing that I could count on every day. . . . I would not be here if it was not for school.

NAOMI, 17

I think rape will never escape my mind, never as long as we have men in this world who are watching MTV.

SONIA, 19

In Berkeley we went to a meeting for gay, lesbian, and bisexual youth at the Pacific Center for Human Growth. It was like a support group. They could all talk about prejudice or anything they wanted to talk about. Naomi was quite outspoken at this meeting. She had a lot of spunk and I thought she'd be a great person to talk to.

The next day, Sunday, she came to my hotel with her friend. I sat on the floor and she sat at the little table with her friend and just talked. I hardly had to ask her anything. She just talked and talked and talked. She poured her heart out and I felt sorry for her the whole time. I didn't get mad at her once the way I did with some of the others. She was just amazing. She's been through so much and yet she's really trying to make something of herself.

She had a pretty gruesome childhood with her stepfather, living on a sailboat, and he beat her. Her mom denies that she and Naomi were beaten by the stepfather.

Her family has turned on her anyhow since she came out and said that she was a lesbian. They have not wanted to have anything to do with her. But she was very open about it. She didn't try to hide it at all. She was being so honest that I didn't think anything like, Uh-oh, what if she comes on to me? She was just very open and honest and nice and polite, and she didn't scare me at all. I was not scared of her and I was not scared of her friend.

She was very short, about five feet one inch, and she had blond hair that was cut very short, shaved on the sides and on the back, and sort of longer on top. It was a nice haircut. She just looked like your average teenager.

She's a recovering alcoholic. She realized that alcohol wasn't going to solve her problems and she really wants to go to college. She's trying to make her life better and worthwhile, even though she doesn't have support from her family. Her whole support is from her friends. She lives on her own, she pays the rent, she pays her bills, she works, and she does all her homework! She was just amazing, a nice, caring, self-confident person. She was captivating.

Sarah Young, 17, Editor

I'm unemployed, I'm poor, I was born on February fifth, Hank Aaron's birthday, and I'm really proud about that. I don't have any brothers or sisters. My mom and dad divorced when I was about three months old and I lived on a boat for years. Unfortunately, we lived much more unhappily than the space on the boat allowed for, but nobody asked me.

I'm a lesbian. That's kind of important. I am happy about that. My favorite movie is *Thelma and Louise,* a truly beautiful movie.

I'm also an alcoholic and I get bored really easily sometimes. I enjoy being bored. I like boredom because it's relatively peaceful, however brain-dead it may seem.

It was awful when I was growing up. There was nothing good about it. On the boat you didn't have space for your own body, you were never alone. I got along with my mom pretty well, to a certain extent, but my stepfather was always telling me I was shit, I could never escape it. He was always saying things like, You're never good enough, you never do what I say, you never do what I say the right way, you never do what I say when I want you to, when I tell you to, the way I tell you to. He always told me to leave and go for a walk: Just get out of my face, out of my sight, you're pitiful.

He's such a strange man, I've never met anybody else like him. I just couldn't rationalize how he could feel this way about me, but we just didn't get along at all and that was a big chunk of my life.

My mom and I were the only ones there, you know, nobody else saw what went on there. But now my mom's denying it and I'm saying, Wait a minute, no, this stuff went on. We shared this experience and we need to stick together, at least emotionally. Ever since I can remember, I thought, even though I was living in this throbbing insanity, I always thought I'd be with my mom. I never thought that at sixteen I'd have to leave my mom and be completely on my own.

The first time I moved out was in August last year when things between my mom and me had gotten really bad. She was treating me and talking to me like my stepfather did. I had been paying for my own therapy for some time then, and going to support groups at school, trying to figure out why I was so unhappy. She didn't want to deal with that.

I was changing and certain stuff wasn't okay for me anymore. That was really pissing her off, and she started getting more and more negative and even violent with me for no reason. One day in August she threw me into a wall, she hit me and gave me a bloody nose and I was like gushing all over the carpet. She barricaded us in her room and wouldn't let me leave. It was really one of the worst things I've ever been through in my life, looking in the mirror and seeing my face and realizing that in my whole life there's been no sense to it. I guess at this point I still hadn't emotionally accepted that my mom was somebody who was really sick and who couldn't take care of me.

I need my mom to just respect me for my brain and whatever it thinks and my thoughts, and I want her to just be really proud of me because she was a witness to everything I've been through. I want her to look at where I am now and who I am and be really proud. I need her to feel a lot better about telling me she loves me, and I need her to do that more often. I need her mostly to just be a friend. I need her not to call and hang up on me even before I've said anything. I mean, I've been my own parent forever and I need her to just treat me like a normal person. I wish she could just hug me when she wanted to.

She seems to feel so awful just talking to me in general. She seems to be really afraid of me. The biggest problem has been that she's denied and lied about the past to my face. Maybe we can do that to the rest of the world, like keep the cover up, but she can't do that with me, you know, I was there. We can't even hurt each other with it because I know her pain and she knows mine.

I'm on my own now and this is the first time in my life I'm really happy about where I live, and that's a real mind-blower because it's hand to mouth, but it's real nice not to have that craziness around.

School was my church, it was my religion. It was constant, the only thing that I could count on every day. There were times, when I first moved out, I wasn't eating at all. I had no money, I was living on beans, I didn't have much. It was really hellish and I was getting sick all the time. Even though I fell asleep in a lot of my classes, I knew I needed to be there and I needed to be falling asleep in that class 'cause I knew what was happening in my body and I knew what was happening to my sanity and I knew it was going to take me a while to adjust again.

It was nice to have that space to do it in, though it was very much within my own brain. I write a lot and that's how I made it, by working through my stuff and doing my algebra homework, even though I didn't know how to do it, because it meant a lot to me that they were giving me homework, like as if I had the possibility of doing it well.

I thought, Wow, maybe I can do something right in my life and other people will know this, too, that I can. So I was very much comforted by school. With my English classes and some of my other classes, it was like, I really don't want to be here this early, but I'm glad I'm here. I enjoy the work and I needed it, I needed it to keep my life focused.

School is a big chunk of my dream, you know. What I'm panicked about now is that I need to find an okay job so I can try to finish my senior year by January and then I can work full time to get money because the college that I want to go to is not cheap.

I would not be here if it was not for school. I had a few really good people in my life that were on the faculty and had known about me ever since I started school. I didn't have to say a word to them, they just knew and they were there for me time and again. It was good to get that kind of acceptance. I would not be here if it hadn't been for school. I'd be very lost.

It gave me such a positive direction for myself, just to feel like I could go somewhere and still do something with myself. At the same time, that was kind of depressing 'cause even though I was doing really well, I couldn't say, Hey Mom, check this out, you know? I couldn't share this stuff with her. I didn't have anybody I could get gushy with about my daily life. And that's important, you know?

I'm excited about school this year. I've waited to be in advanced-placement English for a long time, and I can't wait to mystify my teachers again! I'm looking forward to all of the school part, but I'm definitely not looking forward to the school's population. I wish I could just go there and everybody else didn't exist.

I suppose there's nothing really wrong with them, it's just like your typical high-school thing and I've never fit into it. They know about me, they totally know about me, and I've always been an outcast. I've always at least been funny, which helped me get along, but I've always been real different and real funky and breaking silences a lot.

When they ask me a question, I answer it, whether they want to hear my answer or not. That's really important to me, like my writing, it's a big theme throughout my whole life to break silence, even when nobody wants to hear. That's probably why my writing is so dear to me, because it's a legitimate documentation of me, and people will have to deal with that. That's sort of scary, actually, that's a big, throbbing fear of mine.

I think everybody knows that I'm a lesbian. But there's like different levels of consciousness about it. People at school make a lot of assumptions about it, which is not really a safe thing. It's a very dangerous thing as far as honesty goes. I feel like if they don't know, or didn't know then, they sure will now. By now they've learned the words and they've seen crazy people that they want to associate as typically queer or homosexual. But I don't really give a damn, you know. I really don't. It's exciting for me to know that, too, that I'm still gonna stay true to myself.

It's been a weird transition for me, it's very strange for me to be taking care of me. Not only because I'm seventeen, but because I'm not supposed to do that, I'm supposed to be dependent, but I've said no to that and have been able to work through all of those issues. I've done it mostly completely on my own as far as my self stuff goes and it just blows my mind. I don't understand why I am what I am, but I know I am.

I'm not sure I would change my life, because I wouldn't be what I am or who I am now. I respect the experience I had with my stepfather. I mean it was awful, it was abuse every single day for over a decade, but that's the way it goes. I was powerless over any of it. It was not my choice, but I didn't know how to choose any other way. I couldn't have even if I wanted to. I was only a kid.

My mom was there, she saw the terror in my eyes, she saw everything, but she never tried to stop it. She was oblivious to a lot of things. She doesn't believe my stepfather was an alcoholic, she doesn't believe I'm an alcoholic. That's fine, but I tried to tell her and now it's hard for me to hear from her because I've accepted my disease and I've accepted the way it was for me.

When I drank, I knew that if I drank a lot, I'd be real mellow and morose and unhappy and melancholy and not cool. So when I drank, I drank because I was really upset and feeling awful. I was definitely drinking out of that situation.

Now, with my mom, well, I don't really want to want this from her right now, 'cause it's not possible, it's just out of the question, but if she could only say, Wow, it was a really hard time for both of us and I'm sorry you went through this, Naomi, you have so much potential and you're a good person. I can't imagine her saying something like that about me. Instead she tells me, You're not an alcoholic, but you're a bitch in every other way, there's all this stuff that's wrong with you. That's what she says instead.

Now I have no desire to drink. So much of my life has come to mean so much more to me because I've gotten it together and nobody else was willing to do it for me. That's been a really unique thing for me to realize, which is good. I'm just accepting a lot more about myself and being happy about it instead of feeling shitty about it.

I can't explain what it's been like for me, to have everybody in my family just like be in la-la land and then to have Alateen, where somebody says, Well, Naomi, you're right. You're not crazy. So now I can feel better about telling people how I'm feeling. I don't want to go crazy, I really don't. I've lived very crazily for a long time and that's not what I'm here for.

The most important thing for me now is to be safe. I really hate violence. I just really freak out when I'm in situations that are stemming from irritation, or agitation, or belligerence 'cause I think it's so wrong, it's so unnecessary.

So I want always to have food, I want to write very badly, and I want to get published. I have a lot to say about lots of different things. My three big things in life are women, syntax, and silences. It's like my triumvirate of existence. The silences—I've been shut up all my life, but I've left these little screen tracks here and there in my life and I've always tried to make noise somewhere, tried to be heard.

I'm just now starting to think of the future as something tangible, as something that I have my own power in. That makes me feel really good, so I try to stick with that, wondering about doing something new when I really don't know how it's going to turn out. I want to be happy and I want to leave something behind, I want to do something, I want to change whatever community I'm in.

Sonia is a small and very pretty young woman. She is working to help prevent unnecessary violence through the Resolving Conflict Creatively program at Washington Irving High School in New York City. She is one of the youngest in a large family, so her siblings picked on her often, although she thought it was normal.

She has a very strong character. She is independent and can easily take care of herself. She is what I would call anti-bully. She's the girl who stands up for the underdog. Because the interview was not in private, though, I think she may have held back some feelings.

Sarah Young, 17, Editor

SONIA, 19, NEW YORK CITY

My name is Sonia. I'm half Filipina—my mother's from the Philippines, of Spanish-Indian blood, and my father is American—but my grandfather is white Anglo-Saxon Protestant and my grandmother is a Russian-Polish Jew. So I'm like this mutt.

I was a violent child. My whole family used to fight all the time. I was very violent. I was very quick with my hands. Someone told me once that I was ready to push and shove no matter what happened. I was in karate until I was sixteen and I was very strong. I liked all that physical aggression, and if someone said anything that I didn't like, I was ready to fight about it. I had to be real confident because I was taking karate and I was with all men in a crowded school. I just wanted to get back at people. I wasn't thinking of how I could de-escalate or integrate what other people were doing, so I just picked fights all the time.

Coming from wanting to be in fights all the time, it was hard to come here at first. You know, you got praise for being in fights. And I was proud of it. I used to be proud to come home with bruises, which is really very silly.

Now I would enter a dialogue. I would ask, What's happening here? If the other person was close to me, I'd start walking away, side by side, so that we're not in a confrontational position. What else would I do differently? I definitely would not

87

put the person down. That just increases the level of violence.

I have learned how to do this because I interned with the Resolving Conflict Creatively program when I was at "City as School" High School. It's an alternative high school and that's how I'm able to do this work, earn credit, and be in a unique setting.

We try to decrease violence by learning techniques in active listening, which means paraphrasing, restating the facts, listening nonviolently, not interrupting, not calling someone names, and body language.

We learn the skill of I/eye messages to state how you feel in a way that doesn't put the other person down. We help people articulate how it is they're feeling so they're not saying "You stupid idiot" all the time. So that helps decrease violence and de-escalate what can be potentially violent.

People our age usually are not in the mainstream, but it has to happen more and more. I teach parents, and that gives me confidence and self-esteem. I have the feeling that I can say how I feel and not be ashamed of it, not be afraid to have the feelings that I have. I've also learned to be aware and speak up. I'm far more aware than I was before about subtle messages, subtle innuendos and barriers, breaking down my own barriers, my space.

This program has helped me to see things more openly and more clearly, to appreciate my background and my heritage and being female and being Asian. By learning about one's own culture, we can better understand each other and then, if not appreciate another person or sex or age or culture or sexual orientation, then at least have a tolerance. At least a tolerance.

Through our actions, through our words, we show that we're serious about what we're doing and that we are actual examples of what it is we're talking about. We're modeling a peaceful, nonviolent approach. You can be assertive, too—you're not giving up your values, you're not giving up your way of thinking. You're not giving up anything. But you are learning to *talk* about your differences.

Once you try it out and it works, you go home and say to your mom, Please don't do that to me anymore, I don't like it, and if you get a reaction, you try to do it again. We give the students and ourselves and all the people who work here the tools and safe space and it works.

There is violence all over. Violence is a continuum, from being ignored to psychological abuse to physical abuse to sexual abuse—it's out there. Just walking down the street, a girl gets lots of comments. Someone's looking at you or shouting, Hey, mama, what's up? Hey, *mamasita*. That's violence right there, violence to a woman.

Violence is everywhere. It's in the television, in the newspapers we read, it's in the radio that we listen to, it's in the songs that we hear, it's in everything. There are subtle messages as well as blatant messages, but it's all accepted. It's not questioned. There's no escaping it.

It makes me very scared. I think rape will never escape my mind, never as long as we have men in this world who are watching MTV. I think that I will always fear it. I want to live in a world where I don't have to fear it. I don't want my sisters to fear it, or my nieces. It's not paranoia that we have to be aware and not walk down desolate blocks. It's reality because men are in power. It's men who go out and rape or batter their wives. They're in power, so they're able to do it.

Someone once told me an eye for an eye makes the whole world blind. I think that basically capsulizes what it is that we're trying to express and create and instill. You can't reciprocate hate and violence with hate and violence. You've got to reciprocate instead with love and understanding, because my children would do it to their children and their children would do it to their children, and so on and so forth.

I've seen it for myself. These are my peers, my friends. Even they relate to each other differently, to their situations differently, because they're having open minds and thinking, What could I have done differently? What could I do right now? Everything moves on, not expanding like straight out, but more circular, like a continuum.

As teenagers we have to think about little children; as adults we have to, too. We're young, in a more vulnerable place and less empowered in society, so we have just got to take care of each other.

I keep doing this because I want a world that's safer and better for me and the other people who live in it. Actually, what motivates me is my niece Jessica, who's four years old. She and my niece Jacqueline. When I see them, I know that I don't want this continuum of neglect, abuse, assault to go on, this realm of violence to continue. I don't want them to live in a world like this.

When I see adults changing and redeveloping and relearning and everything, that helps motivate me, too, because I feel proud and think, If they can do it, so can we. A lot of it comes out of anger, too. When something is horrible, I get angry and anger motivates me. So I just say, Stop it, I don't want this to happen anymore.

But sometimes it's hard to be motivated when everything seems to be coming down. A lot of times I feel down, too, but when you experience the level of humanity that I've been experiencing doing this work, then I want to do even more.

I feel like I'm making a difference. At first I just wanted to change masses of people, but I know first you have to change and be open to change yourself. I think what helps make a difference is just relating to people differently. I'm listening a lot more and I'm trying to be nonjudgmental about it, especially if it's something that I don't agree with. So I'm learning to listen and that's breaking down yet another violent act, when people are constantly interrupted or told that they're wrong or some other thought is interjected.

I'm making a difference in my life because I feel better about myself. As I begin to empower myself, others are doing it as well. I see it more when the children do it, when my little cousins, my nieces and nephews, do it. They feel safe, I know they feel safe around me.

I'm not thinking any more of how I can manipulate someone or get them back. I'm not thinking vengefully. I'm still an angry youth, I'm angry at what goes on in our world. This violence, this abuse, this shouldn't be happening. We shouldn't be living like this. There's no reason why we should live like this, living to exploit. Exploitation is violence. We shouldn't have to, there's no reason for it, and there are alternatives.

So we're learning creative conflict resolution. One time there was a fight when I was going to the train station and I started singing. I just started singing at the top of my lungs. People were wondering, What's going on here? What's she singing for? And it stopped. These people stopped fighting. They had just been thunderously pounding and pummeling each other on the ground, and here I am singing.

You need a crowd to egg you on. When you hear everyone cheering, you're overcome with it, so it becomes you. But when the crowd started dispersing and looking at me like this crazy person singing, they needed that. Afterwards, they were kind of arguing, but they weren't physically hurting each other anymore. So I've learned to be more creative, too.

It's really up to us to make a difference. It's up to every person individually to make a collective difference. We don't have to live this way, if we just stop thinking for ourselves in a selfish way. It's good to think for yourself, but when you just want to exploit another, that's violence.

Even just *listening* to someone is like changing. To be honest is changing, to have an open mind is changing. It's very little things that matter. To try to believe in yourself, which is hard with all the messages that we get, that's changing. We really need to work hard together and support each other because we can't do it alone. That way is just futile.

Gang members.

GANGS

They were willing to scare me and I was willing to kill them. It didn't scare me that they had a gun. Because I was willing to die.

TWACE, 21

I have a buddy that shot his own father for the gang—you do a lot of stuff.

ROBERT, 17

Accident

A   T r u e   S t o r y

---

it was a longtime
and this Boy Name Steve
got shot on 14 Street   .
and when he got shot
he tried to get up
But everytime he try to get up
they kept shooting him
I start crying
and his mother was crying two
and girlfriend had A nervousbreakdown

PHYLLIS LOMAX, 11

Twace was dying to tell his story. So he told it. They say when someone tells a long story you're supposed to fall asleep, but I was wide awake because his things are real.

He's a big, tall guy who's kind of scary looking, the way he looks at people and acts. He has tattoos. Sometimes he lets his hair grow on the top, sometimes he cuts it short. He was wearing a black vest—an outlaw vest—leather. His ethnic background is Puerto Rican. He gets a lot of respect and he has a lot of respect.

He's mean and tough 'cause he went through a lot of hard stuff, man. I felt sad in a way because I've known him for a long time and I just don't want to see anything happen to him. But he told me that he did heroin, everything in the book. He's bugged out.

He said he wants to read the book and I know he's reading it right now, so I'd just like to tell you, Twace, from the bottom of my heart, I don't want nothing happening to you. I don't want to see you go away, you know, do stupid things. Just keep trying, man. Please. You can make it if you try.

Eric Zamora, 16, Editor
with Rolando Liriano, 16, Editor

TWACE, 21, BROOKLYN

How are you doin'?! My name is Twace, and I'm twenty-one years old right now. I first started using drugs, joining gangs, and running with the crowd when I was about nine years old.

I was running with clubs and stuff like that 'cause that gives you some kind of respect. But it was really kind of hard. Respect is something that you could lose at any moment, you know, you could lose it to stupidity. Sometimes I'm scared of myself because I know a few motherfuckin' things, from a gun to a knife. So sometimes it scares me, but it's the only way I know how to be.

I was going to a school where all these kids are crazy, everybody's using drugs, and you want to fit in. So by the time I went to junior high school I was already thirteen years old and I was somebody. I eventually ended up stabbing somebody, ended up shooting somebody and using drugs. I'm right now currently recovering from being a junkie.

It's not something I'm proud of, but it's the honest truth, I'm a recovering addict. I'm still going through the phases, you know, because I started from marijuana to pills to drinking to hallucinates to heroin to cocaine to crack. I did every kind of drug you'll ever think of. And all of this was just to fit in, you know, just to fit in, to be cool. It sounds kind of stupid and it sounds like, Well, if you know that's what you gotta do, then why did you do it? It's just because it's part of the way the neighborhood is and the way you feel you gotta be. I mean I look at young guys nowadays and I say, Damn, man, don't start something you can't finish.

Something like I've started, you cannot ever finish. I know guys that are three times my age and are still the same way, you know. They're bikers or they're just plain-out junkies or they're ex-cons. Why? Because they don't know nothing else. Because they closed their minds. And that's what we're doing. We're closing our minds. That's the way we live and that's the way we'll die. So I went to school and I was already a murderer and this carried a lot of weight. I was somebody, all the girls liked me, man. I was a little king to all those girls.

Then I started getting into heavier stuff. And this is all because of the reputation. This is all 'cause you want to be somebody, because you gotta be down. Your name has gotta ring. And if your name don't ring, you ain't nobody.

By the time I was fifteen I already had a tattoo, something that broke my mother's heart, but I didn't care, I was so psyched up on being crazy I had to get it, you know what I mean? To this day I keep getting them because it's just the way I am, you know. I keep thinking, I still think the way I thought back then. I gotta prove something, that's why I do it mainly.

You know, everybody who had a reputation, somebody follows him so they can be somebody, so I carried a lot of people, man. I carry a lot of people to this day. I got hurt, I've been arrested, I've been in jail for protecting a lot of different people.

I started popping pills like crazy. I started doing a lot of 'ludes, a lot of quaaludes. I mean, I didn't even know what I was on, I was so wiped out of my head. I just did it because I liked the way I looked when I was high—I looked like I was a maniac, I looked like I was crazy. Nobody would dare fuck with me. I used to go to school, the teachers were scared of me, you know. I rang bells. I got through two junior high schools because of fear. The principals used to fear me, the police used to fear me. It was all because I had to prove something and I was willing to prove it even if I got killed.

Even to this day, sometimes I be scared of myself, because I could be killed at any time or moment just because I don't give a flying fuck because I can't be disrespected. I can't be disrespected and that's the way I live.

Then I switched schools and one day I see these guys walking past and they dared my cousin and I said, Yo, man, you dare me to be down with them people? I'll give you five minutes. And he was like, Yeah, I dare you. So I went over and I joined them. I had to whack the shit out of some guy with a chain. I mean I almost killed the guy.

I almost killed the poor guy, but then after that it was all right, I was down with the posse. Mutual respect again like I needed it, you know what I mean? I joined the club because I needed the respect. Wherever I went I didn't want nobody to bother me, and the only club in this school that had everybody in control was these people. So I run down with them.

This is when I started doing the heaviest drugs there is. It's heroin and I'm only fifteen years old. I usually say it was the love of my life. But, you know, you think 'cause you look down, and you think 'cause you look crazy, people will respect you, but they just scared of you, it's not respect. It's just being scared. Plain bloody scared.

When you're on these missions, people are just scared of you, but it's not because they look at that dude and say, Oh, man, I respect this guy. This guy did this. This guy helped this person. This guy helped build this. You know. Nah, if anything, I might help somebody tear something down and do something to somebody. To hurt them. It's all fear. It's all fear. I mean at times it feels good, sometimes, but sometimes it doesn't.

One day, I was by myself with this girl. These guys tell her, What you doing with this spick? And that blew my mind. I turned around and I said, Yo, man, she's walking with me, what's up? So one of them comes and cracks me in the head with a bottle. So I don't know where the other two people are, I told my girl to just run. In those days it was jumbo knives, they came in a case, they were in style, I had one. And the case wouldn't open. So I started running. There were three of them. They were coming at me with some heavy shit, you know. So I'm running. Now one of them catches up to me and he was a jock, and I was already drugged up. I couldn't run the block. He comes and jumps over me with his leverage, his pull. I ended up opening the knife, the case. I flipped over 'cause I'm quick with a blade like it ain't nothing. And I stabbed him right in the side and there's another guy came behind me and I stabbed him in his leg. And this is happening about a block away from my house. Then some old ladies, white old ladies, while they were beating me up, it was all right. They wouldn't call the police. But when I started sticking them, then it was okay to call police, so police started coming and I started breaking out. I broke out. That was the second time I stabbed somebody.

Then I got out of there, and I went to junior high school. In those days it was crews. The gangs were already out of style, so it was all crews. This crew, that crew, stupidity, you know. There was a lot of jams at that time. I went in and I made a crew. I was the Prez this time, I was the leader. I had my soldiers, I had my warriors, and I had my officers. We even had a club, you know: You come to my club and you buy these drugs, you buy this liquor; if not, you would get a beating.

One time, I was seventeen and I was coming from work. I'm not lazy, I do like to work. I work when I have to. This time I had a car, so I had to work. I had to afford the gas and all that stuff. And I had this girl, it's when I first had my kid. So I'm driving and I see this dude from a club that I didn't like. This was something that went back to when I was thirteen years old. I see this guy with his arm wrapped around my little sister, and I drive up. I'm carrying a bag. You carry a bag in case you have a problem with somebody.

I pick up the bag, he gives me a smile, like what am I going to do. What am I going to do? I'm a guy who's being raced up, being respected. Nobody will look at my face, nobody will smile at my face unless I am smiling. Nobody would even talk to me unless I talked to them. Now this guy goes smiling in my face. First thing I react to was to kill him, you know what I mean? You gonna laugh at me, I'm gonna kill you. And that's basically what I almost did.

The guy was in a coma for a little while, you know. They came after me a few times, they blew up my car and all that stuff, and I came back, you know, they pulled out guns and I was so whacked out, I actually chased the guy, the guy with a .45 and I'm with a bat. And I almost killed the motherfucker. I was so whacked out. They were willing to scare me and I was willing to kill them. It didn't scare me that they had a gun. Because I was willing to die.

This is because I was just raised like this, you know. This being respected stuff is really what's fucking up this world. The youth of the world. 'Cause it's everywhere, this is not just me, you know. This is a problem with everybody. It's not just me, it's not just this neighborhood, it's every neighborhood, from blacks to Puerto Ricans to white boys to Chinks to everything. There's always got to be a leader.

Always got to be a leader and I was willing to be the leader. Sometimes my brothers, my homeboys, my friends, they would say, Twace, you gotta chill out, 'cause one day you're gonna get killed. There's going to be a guy who maybe is crazier than you who's going to take you out.

I didn't care. I didn't give a flying fuck, you know. To this day I'd be scared of myself because I know how I am. The problem is having this respect, this thing we're supposed to have. When I look at my father or my uncles and stuff, they don't act the way I act. They never been down with that. I didn't play tag and all that shit. I thought that was for punks. What I was doing was crazy, way crazier. The people I ran with wasn't doing stupidities like that. I figured it was stupid—hide-and-go-seek, playing tag, man hunting, and all this kiddie shit. I mean I don't even know how to play that stuff. I don't know nothing about playing football or basketball or baseball 'cause I never spend no time with it. I spend time with my self-rep, you know, building up my reputation.

The first time I really got locked up, I was fifteen years old. I was using heroin, but nobody knew it. I knew it, and the people I copped off of. When I used heroin, I sniffed it, and it was pure, it rocked my bells. I loved it, so I started selling weed and that first day I sold it I got busted.

I said, Well, this is my first time I've ever been arrested, first time through the system. I go in there and they told me, Listen, you gonna get two to six. Man, I was so mad that day. I was cursing every stupidity. Every day, I'm looking at the D.A. dirty, man, I was scared, I was nervous. My lawyer's telling me, Don't look at the D.A. like that, 'cause I wanted to kill him. Eventually I ended up doing ninety days. I went to jail. It was the worst fear of my life.

You know, I had already ripped people up for a pair of lousy sneakers, for food, whatever. For anybody whoever hears this, if you think what I'm saying ain't nothing compared to what you did, believe me, homeboy, ain't nothing you done or anybody can do any better than what I did, man. And I regret every bit of it.

In jail, Puerto Rican is German. German mean Nazi, like outlaw, crazy motherfucker, willing to cut anybody up, willing to just kill somebody. And the people I was with, they were punks, Puerto Rican guys I was with were punks. So I was on my own basically, sixty-some guys to a dorm. I had to rip a couple of people up, you know. And after that people were doing me stuff, people begging me so they can clean my clothes for a cigarette.

When you're in there, you got to have the respect you had in the street. Because you could be—I mean, the guys that were in prison were nothing but a bunch of suckers. And out here they thought they were hot shit. To this day they see me and they don't even look at me because they're degraded, you know.

Time came I went home and everything. Everything went smooth, after three weeks I was living large. I mean, I came out of there big fat, you know what I mean. I gave all my clothes out and all that stuff, I gave my sneakers away, you know. Had things I didn't need.

Came home and the same thing was still waiting for me out here. Same people. Everything. This time I came out, had a good girl, she handled all my bullshit. I come out and again this thing starts with the white boys. They don't see me for a little while, they figure, Ah, let's fuck this guy again. See if he's got it in him. They come by my house, see if I got beat up while I was in there. They look at me, they shocked 'cause I didn't care, you could have killed me and I didn't give a flying fuck. Jail, streets, anywhere, you know.

So I was all right. Happy feeling there, you know, finally had another kid. Have another daughter. Time went by and I ended up using drugs all over again. I was lifting weights. Started using drugs and building myself up. *Boom.* Became a junkie. This time it was no more about being respected. I mean I was a junkie and I was respected 'cause people would think back, Man, if he was this crazy way back, he's crazy now, you know what I mean, 'cause you can't be a punk once and be a bad motherfucker again. I mean you a bad motherfucker, or you just ain't. I was the meanest junkie that was around here. I would have robbed anybody, stabbed anybody, shot anybody, in a matter of a heartbeat. Heroin is something very big. It's not a dictator of your mind, it's a dictator of your body.

I started selling drugs. Started being big-time. I had money coming out of my ass. I had jewelry, I had everything I could

101

ever want. So I started using like crazy. *Boom.* Started using and using and using until I got hooked on it and went to the hospital, a detox. Then when I came back out, started using again.

This is something that my respect brought me to, you know. To becoming a heroin addict. I'm not proud of it, but I'm also not ashamed of it. I figure it was something that I had to go through to learn what life was really about, you know.

So when I say I'm a junkie, I don't say I'm degraded or nothing like that, 'cause it was something I went through. It was something that I had to do, and as long as you live through it, it was all right. Not all right, but you made it. I'm in recovery right now, so I ain't got nothing to be ashamed of, you know.

Then I married a decent girl. We still hanging in there. We got a son together, you know. That's my little nigger. For that little nigger, man, I'd give more than my life, because what I went through he'll never go through, I hope to God. I hope that what I've gone through will serve him as an example to go to school and do the right thing.

I got my son and I think about him a lot. I think about him and I be scared, I be scared a lot. I'll be damned, boy, I hope this little nigger doesn't go through not even half or a quarter of the things I went through, 'cause I love him to nuts, I love him to pieces. There ain't nobody could ever do anything to that little guy. I just don't want him to go through what I went through.

And I lost him, too, you know, right now I don't even got him. I was too fucked up in my mind, I guess, to have him around me. But he's got it all right, he's having a lot of fun out there, with flowers and stuff like that. But we ain't together, and I miss him. Soon we will be. I look better now, I don't use drugs. I'm not using drugs.

To this day I wish that something I say will scare somebody away from doing what I did, man, 'cause what I did wasn't worth it. I spent my whole childhood, my whole childhood in and out of prison. I was high out of my head. I had a lot of friends I grew up with, but the only one who ever gave me drugs was me. And this was because I had to be somebody, somebody that people respected, man.

That's the bottom line, *boom*, for every whopper [important person] out there there's a tomb, for every whopper there's a cell, for every whopper out there there's a drug's box [coffin]. 'Cause there's only three ways you going, man: You going to jail, you going to be killed, or you're going to be a dope fiend, crackhead, whatever it is, because it's all in the game. It's all in the game of this respect bullshit. I look at my elders, man, they never went through stuff like this, 'cause they didn't have to prove nothing to nobody. In those days it was, I don't know, I really can't say what it was like in those days, but it sure in hell was better than it is now, man.

I wish to God somebody would have spoke up to me and said, Yo, kid, do this like this. Get yourself a job and do things the right way and you'll be better off. 'Cause I had all of that—I had cars, I had drugs, I had money, I had girls, I had everything I could ever want—and to this day right now, right now what am I doing? I'm working and I'm trying to fight being an addict because I don't want to be an addict all my life.

This is all because I wanted to be bad. I wanted to be a part of the crew, be down with everybody. And look at all it got me. All it got me was going to jail, hooked on drugs. I got three kids, God bless them, but I can't afford them.

You gotta do the right thing, and the right thing is just going to school, man, and be listening to your parents, they got a lot of knowledge.

I've learned it the hard way. If I did have somebody to guide me, maybe I wouldn't have been like this, you know. But I never did. And that's getting a little too heavy, so I won't get into all of that.

Thank God I was one of those who didn't end up being life in prison or dead. Or a junkie. I ended up being one of those that took the path, took a step on the other side, and now he's trying that out. Don't do drugs, man. Don't try drugs 'cause they something nobody can handle.

Despite prepared lists of questions, we were scared. We later learned that we were not the only nervous ones. Even though we were the same ages and lived in the same city, Robert and Ralph were as leery of us as we were of them.

By listening to Robert and Ralph and observing, we entered the cautious, defensive world of gang members, where the rules and dangers of their society were entirely different from any we had previously known. To be a member of a gang means to be bound for life. It means family bound not by blood but by turf, by rank and by loyalty.

For many inner-city kids, including Ralph and Robert, gangs like the Vice Lords or the Disciples are the only tangible family they know. Like families, gangs supply members with food, clothing, shelter, role models, and protection. But unlike most families, there is a cost for this security. Payment involves gang fights and battles (gang banging) that often land brothers in detention homes, jails, hospitals, or morgues.

Wendy Potasnik, 17
Kathleen Hustad, 17
Michelle Evans, 16
Editors

RALPH, 16, INDIANAPOLIS

I was only eight years old when I really got into the gang. When I joined, a lot of older people was gang banging, and joining seemed like the right thing to do. You would get more respect if you were in the gang.

In my neighborhood, this school is known for Disciples. Ain't no Vice Lords gonna go there. If it's a group of us and it's a group of them—if they're over in our territory and we are over in theirs, we got to fight. We got to shoot. We got to do something, because that's how it is.

It's just about selling drugs in school, really. That's what gangs do. Sell drugs in school. Watch their territory.

Where I'm from, you have got a choice. But if you want to fit in and, you know, have a lot of power and run with all those girls looking at you like, He's in a gang . . . I want to get with him, things like that, you don't have much choice.

Young people, they just feel, I guess I can have some power and have a lot of respect around the school. So I guess they just join the gang. But some people just do it because a friend is in it, then they find out that they don't want to be in it. They just can't get out.

If you try to get out of a gang, there's usually a beating—brutal beating—to the hospital or a bullet to the head. Can't be done.

If somebody's over me, over my life, I take the bullet for him. That's the rule. If somebody under me, I ain't going to take the bullet for him. I won't die for anybody that's under me.

You're going always to be in it, but if there comes a time when you're older and you got the upper hand, you ain't gotta do nothing. You sit back and order the people that are assigned to you.

There's times, like in my nation, for me to slow down. Say I have a kid—I still be with it, but there's times for me to slow down and be with my family. I wouldn't have as much as everybody else is doing because I got a little son to raise up and be like me. Families are very important.

ROBERT, 17, INDIANAPOLIS

When I got in they beat me up, you know. They took me out on little missions and stuff like that—having you do little things. Drive-bys [drive-by shootings]. I broke in houses, stores, and stuff like that.

We fight for turf. It would be like everywhere you go they give you respect. There go the Vice Lords. We better walk another way.

If I am by myself and it's a group of Disciples, for me to gain more respect, it's best for me to go at them. Instead of turning and running, like he ain't nothing. He's just a punk. He shouldn't be down with no gang.

First thing that goes through my mind—I hope I make it

through this. If I get shot, I just hope it ain't the one that kills me.

If it's one-on-one, I am going to try to creep on him. If I'm low and I want to gain respect, I am supposed to take him off or do something to hurt him real bad. Then I go back to my neighborhood and probably my fellas already heard about it and then that's more respect.

To me, we're all just one big family. They're just like my brothers. I feel and hope I'd die for them and they'd die for me if it came to it. It's just got that thick after all those years.

You move up in the gang a lot of ways. You can shoot, you can stab, break in stuff, steal things. I have a buddy that shot his own father for the gang. You do a lot of stuff.

If I had a little brother, I'd try to tell him different 'cause I wouldn't want him to go through what I've been through. It wouldn't be right—but it's his own mind.

As I walked through the silent corridors of Boys School, I glanced out the window at a single-file line of boys. As they were being escorted to the adjoining building, the enforcement, the rules—no talking or moving without permission—was evident.

Sitting in a large classroom with three of these young males and taking out my tape recorder, I felt a nervous twitch as the security guard in the back of the room gave me a reassuring glance.

I told these inmates a little bit about myself and they reciprocated by stating their names and their crimes just as natural as I had told them my hobbies.

Chuck laughed in a nervous fashion as he rubbed his dark face with his muscular arms. Derrick, a burly inmate with glasses, egged Chuck on while pushing back his overgrown hair. They hadn't known each other before their sentencing, but their participation in gangs gave them a common bond.

Reggie sat a few feet away from them, symbolically removing himself from the group. The others mocked his large frame and soft style, while he tried hard to be like the other guys. Peer pressure was probably the same reason why he carried a weapon to school, sentencing him to Boys School.

By the end of the interview, I forgot about the security guard as I chatted with these gentle boys, because in talking with them, they were transformed into different people.

Chuck wasn't the rough, tough, street-smart kid who killed three people; Derrick didn't display the typical pushy drug-dealer stereotype, and Reggie's gullible soft style made him appear to be an innocent kid trapped at the wrong place at the wrong time.

In here they are soon forgotten with average stays of about three months. Out on the streets, they are forced to take on a role for their gang, because for them, it's the only family they have.

Robin Potasnik, 15, Editor

DERRICK, CHUCK, AND REGGIE, INDIANAPOLIS

CHUCK: When I was growing up, I say when I was twelve or thirteen, I used to see a lot of gun movies and Western movies.

And I'd see how big the guns were and I'd be like, Man, I bet that would put a hole in a chest or something. I always wanted to know how it feels or how they look if you shoot somebody. I used to just thrive on violence.

When I turned fifteen, that was when I learned my first lesson. I was fighting and I shot somebody. He didn't die. I got all that off of TV because I wanted to see what a bullet hole could do to you, and I never seen nobody get shot before.

REGGIE: I can walk in my school and you'll see kids getting into fights, see kids getting stabbed. You can hear gunshots outside the school. I'm on the West Side, where the cops don't even drive by the schools anymore. It's not even worth their time.

There's violence everywhere all the time. And if you don't see it yourself, flip on the TV and you'll see it on the news.

DERRICK: I get with my homeboys, we just gotta go do something. We walk around school and we see somebody wearing our wrong colors we gonna get him.

We experience violence every day. We just do. You're gonna experience it if you're in a gang 'cause you gotta prove to your homeboys that you're down for what's yours. We gotta prove ourselves down for our boys and our boys gotta prove themselves down to us. You're always gonna be lower than somebody in rank, and you gotta prove to the higher rank that you're really down for your king.

CHUCK: I've seen a lot of my friends die in a gang fight that I was in which it could've been me. Like one of my friends died for a gang fight when I was supposed to fight the boy, but he wanted to fight him because he was big and stuff. He wanted to show that he was down. So he ended up fighting him, and he took the bullet for me. The bullet was supposed to be mine.

I've been doing a lot of thinking here that I should move and just leave it all alone, change my life around. Get away from all the bad stuff. Come back and be an example instead of a dead role model.

DERRICK: If you want to get out of the gang, you ain't gonna get out unless you take three bullets to the head and three to the chest. That's the only way you gonna get out. You gonna die to get out. There's no way. Once you're in, you gotta love your nation. You gotta love, make, hate, and take. You hate the Vice Lords, so you take their life. That's part of our literature. There's no way to get out of a gang safe.

REGGIE: Talk. If they don't pull out the guns and pull out the knives and throw the stuff at people, and they cool off and they think about it and they talk about it, a lot of the stuff that happens wouldn't happen.

DERRICK: But Reggie, listen:
If there's gangs, there's gonna be gang violence. That's what gangs thrive off of is violence. Somebody's always wanting to cross the line sometime and then they gonna have to pay the price if they cross it. If they're by themselves, they're gone. They're gonna get killed.

If you got a bad family, like my family, I can't go home to my mom. I can't sit down and talk to my mom. I gotta go out and do something. When I go up to my friends, that's the only family I got, and they feed off violence. It's like taking a drug—once you get on a drug and you keep on taking it, you're addicted. They're addicted to violence, and I'm addicted to violence, too. I know when I leave here I'll most likely be back for my third time or my fourth. I just know. That's the way it is.

CHUCK: If there were more jobs, I think the crime rate would stop right there because the people would be trying to make their money instead of stealing it and lying and cheating for it

109

and killing people. Get more jobs—that would be the solution. They wouldn't need no Boys School and no prisons except for the people that really wanted to kill somebody. So they'd probably need one open for that.

REGGIE: Get rid of the drugs. A lot of violence comes from drugs. Turn away from it.

4

Turf and Terror: You Ain't One of Us

RACISM

I'm not racist or nothing like that, but I know what time it is. I'm not saying I hate white people, 'cause I don't hate white people. I hate the things that they have done.

FRANKLIN, 17

I expect all nonwhites and Jews and homosexuals to hate me. That's a given. But when white people hate me, that really bugs me a lot.

STORM TROOPER STEVE, 19

Sometimes when I am walking down the street and there are old ladies and old men looking scared, like checking their wallets, it bothers me 'cause I never stole anything in my whole life. Never. And I'm not planning to.

EDWIN, 21

All Alone

I'm so all alone,
Trapped in darkness . . .
Others whispered dark thoughts,
>   *about me under their breaths.*
As I dispersed from the crowd
I shake away my tears that fall like
>   *rain drops*
Voices grow louder bleating out words
>   *towards me . . .*
The hatred that blinds me; hopelessly
>   *making peace with others;*
My heart is heavy with burden;
The ground that is wet with my tears
And my hands that tremble with sorrow
>   *and fear . . .*
I sit alone thinking . . .
I weep away the night,
For tomorrow will be the same;
More angry faces will shout words
>   *that offend me . . .*

ANTHONY SOLIN, 14

I spoke to Franklin at a shopping mall called the Atlanta Underground. He had dark-colored skin. He was black. He dressed like the style over in New York—baggy jeans, baggy shirt, the hoodlum look.

He was talking about violence and all of a sudden he pointed out a man robbing a lady's purse, right in the middle of our interview, and then a cop came and tackled the man down. So I could see, right there in the Underground, how bad it is.

He also talked about how the black and the white are getting taken over by the devil. But I didn't feel that he'd been taken by the devil. He knows what's up. He's not a racist. He looks like a hoodlum, but he's really smart inside. I think he's going to be very successful in life.

Eric Zamora, 16, Editor
with Rolando Liriano, 16, Editor

FRANKLIN, 17, ATLANTA

I come from New York, but I've been down to Atlanta for about a year. Man, shit be happening down here. Crazy-ass shit. When I was in New York, we had schools that was kind of mixed. But when I came down here, they opened up this new school and they had a big old fucking fight with white people against black people just because they was white and black. I was all in the middle of that, but I wasn't hittin' nobody because that war is in your mind, it's not physical.

When I was a child, my father was with me. I guess you could say I had kind of a good childhood compared to all these other kids out here. They kept me sheltered from a lot of stuff, you know, kept me in the house for a long time. Until we got down here I wasn't really hanging out real late.

But in New York, it's real bad. You know, niggers be shooting every night, doing ruthless, bad stuff. When I was there Thanksgiving they shot this kid, unloaded the gun on his head. Thanksgiving. Because he was selling weed. He wanted to get out of the business. And they shot him. I knew him. He had a baby on the way.

My mother never married after my dad left. But it didn't

bother me that much because she act like the man and the woman. I mean she was out there bringing home the bread, you know, whupping our ass when we wasn't doing right, and then she was real loving, too. Like when we needed somebody to uplift us, she was there to give us a helping hand. I guess God is looking out for me. I do believe I'm chosen. He looking out for me.

This new school ain't nothing compared to New York 'cause the white kids, they try to stay to their business. It's still segregated, you know, it's still segregated. They try to say that it's not, but the white kids stay on one side of the hall and the black kids is on the other side of the hall. Even when you go in class, the white kids sit on one side of the class and the black kids is on another. But in New York, niggers getting shot in school over girls and stupid stuff like that.

I heard it got worse, too, up in New York because since I moved down here I know about four or five people got shot and died. Got killed since I've been down here. So it's getting worse.

School in New York was all right for me, except when I left, I got caught. Niggers used to threaten me with guns and stuff, and stupid-ass me, I'd bring a knife instead of a gun and I got caught with the knife. Lucky I didn't bring a gun, I guess, 'cause I know I would have got caught with the gun and I would have been sent to jail, but I left New York instead.

You know, we can't say, Well, it's society's fault, society did this shit to me. If society give you a gun, it's up to you whether or not you're going to use that gun. You know what I'm saying? It's up to you to say, Well, am I going to go out here and shoot this nigger or am I going to just put it down? It's always up to you.

Down here the only kind of violence I really see is in the school when that racial shit happens. But you hear about that shit on the news and it be real sad when you hear about niggers getting shot execution style, fifteen and fourteen years old, for drugs.

Remember that kid that got shot last week? They say he had a bullet through his eye, but he was still alive and the cop said, Well, we not going to call the ambulance because this is just going to be another dead drug dealer. And that's fucked up when life don't mean shit.

When I was in New York I knew a kid fourteen years old got stabbed by a kid fifteen years old. They used to be real good friends. And he stabbed the kid for his Nintendo and VCR. Came up to his door and said, Hey, man, give me your VCR and your Nintendo. And the kid said, Hell no, turned his back on him, and he took that knife and he stabbed him. His parents found him on the floor with a knife through his chest. He was one of those people that never did nothing to nobody, don't know shit about the streets or nothing. That's how he was. That's fucked up when we don't think of nobody's life but for a VCR and a TV. I'm ashamed. That's fucked up.

Me, I read a lot and I got to start praying again. I be praying sometime, but you know, I stopped and I need to start back up again 'cause that really what leaves a lot of the tension. You get your mind off things and try to do for you and your people. There ain't nobody else gonna do for you but yourself.

Now, on the racial stuff, I'm a separatist. I don't believe in integration. I believe Martin Luther King fuck us up when he mixed us with white people. I mean they're some good white people. I ain't saying that all of them is all fucked up and everybody white is bad, but on the whole they fuck people of color up, you know what I'm saying?

All people of color, they came out of the cage and then they wanted to rule the world. And that's what they doing. They rule three-fourths of the world. Now, we don't want to say we gonna take over the world and put the white man in slavery. Then we be just as dirty as he is. So we do it and we rule everything equally, with equality. You know that's what peace stands for. Please Educate All Children Equally.

The white man let the devil use him too much, and it's a lot of black people that let the devil use them too much, too. And that fucks everybody up in the whole world. I gotta change that, 'cause we all chosen. We all chosen to do something down here on Earth. I ain't sitting here waiting to die to go to heaven neither, 'cause I don't believe in heaven and I don't believe in hell. That's all a state of mind. It's all in your mind. We in hell right now. What else can this be? This sure ain't no damn paradise. We in hell and we gotta create a heaven on Earth.

Who in power now? The white people in power. And now we got sheer hell, we got pure, unadulterate hell. When black people was ruling the Earth, we had heaven, you know what I'm saying? And that's what we need, the black man need to rule the Earth again. I'm not racist or nothing like that, but I know what time it is. I'm not saying I hate white people, 'cause I don't hate white people. I hate the things that they have done.

Just like we have slavery in our genes, they have that taskmaster in their genes. Even if they don't want to do it consciously, they want to do it subconsciously, just like black people want to be slaves subconsciously. White people want to be our taskmasters. Actions speak louder than words. Look at history and look at today. People can't see that there's hope for black people.

As it is now, everybody is just dog eat dog. Everybody is going for self and that's what's fucking up everybody because everybody is not concerned about the group. Everybody's worried about number one. I'm number one. I got to do this, I got to do that, I, I, I, I. . . . What about everybody else?

If I had three wishes? This is totally unrealistic, but if people could just get along, like they claim heaven is going to be, I would wish for some shit like that. And with that wish all wishes would come manifested. If you just wish for that, for peace and tranquillity in everybody's life, for everybody to get along, all wishes will succeed. It's really only one wish.

During the daytime, you don't see the underside of the city. It's the nighttime when you find drug addicts, runaways, skinheads.

It was tough to interview a skinhead. I had to separate myself and hide my own views in order not to stifle Storm Trooper Steve's desire to talk.

The strange thing is that I started to feel that he was actually a nice guy. I could see a person buying into his rhetoric. It was scary to realize that people who think so differently can still be similar, or even likable, to you.

Shane Tilston, 17, Editor

STORM TROOPER STEVE, 19, SAN FRANCISCO

When people ask me why I'm doing what I'm doing, it's so obvious. Whenever I walk around San Francisco, it's just *wham!* Now I know why I'm a skinhead, because San Francisco is so fucking gross. I'm living in your faggot capital of the universe and I'm living it up. I'm partying it up.

But no one likes me. Everyone hates skinheads. People come out in packs to beat us. I'm constantly getting death threats on my message machine. Black gangsters from everywhere have put hits on me. I have enough contracts on my head that there's certain neighborhoods I just won't go into anymore.

But I love it. I totally enjoy it. I know you guys hate me, too. A lot of people have tried to take me out, but I'm a real survivalist type. I have people who have put guns on me, try to stab me, and I'm still standing here, so I guess I'm doing something right. They've yet to succeed.

Every culture except for modern-day western culture in the past hundred and fifty years or so has had a caste in society where the warrior was given a position of honor. I feel like skinheads are the warrior class in a society that neither understands nor appreciates a warrior class. So people don't understand us, they're terrified of us 'cause the media portray us as violent.

We are violent people because we are so angry all the time,

because my kinfolk are being destroyed. The white race is being eroded. And the worst part about that is I'm defending kinfolk that don't want to be defended.

I expect all nonwhites and Jews and homosexuals to hate me. That's a given. But when white people hate me, that really bugs me a lot. I'm obviously not making money doing this. But it's so rare that a white person will go, Damn straight, Steve, you did a good job.

I'm willing to take the persecutions because I know what I'm doing is right. Time and time again I'll see something, like black people will do the exact things that we stereotype them as. The drive-by shootings. You know, typical nigger activity. This ex-girlfriend and I were going to get a burrito, and on this park bench there was this pile of watermelon rinds and we were like, Gee, who could have been here? Total Amos and Andy type thing. Buckwheat would have been proud.

Time and time again people get mad at us for stereotyping Jews as being greedy. I've yet to meet a nonmiserly Jew. I've had so many Jewish bosses who are nasty and rude and cheap. That's part of their culture, but you're not supposed to say that.

The reason I say we're supremacists is because no other culture has done what western culture has done. While my ancestors were making cars and televisions, their ancestors were putting bones through their noses. Africans were still making mud huts while the Japanese were making these beautiful silk screens and fine swords out of metal.

The Japanese—even though they're my enemy—I have a lot of respect for them because we should be doing what they're doing. They have it down pat. Discipline. Family oriented. Racially homogenous business culture. They don't allow blacks and Jews in, period.

I really think it encourages mediocrity for the superior to help the inferior. I don't believe in charity, like feeding people in Bangladesh. Feeding them just keeps them alive longer. And they're not producing anything. They're just detracting from us.

The swift should not have to slow down for the lame. Survival of the fittest, you know. If I can evolve higher than you, I'm not going to stunt my growth to help you catch up with me. It just encourages weakness to keep all those starving people alive. People who were born handicapped or retarded are a drag. If a wolf cub is born with some deformity, the mom just chucks it out.

My parents are very nice, fundamentalist Baptist people. Jerry Falwell was their hero. Honest to God. I was encouraged to send some of my allowance to him and I did. But then, around fourteen or fifteen, I just really thought Christianity was a load of shit and I've been an atheist ever since.

My parents are so all-American it's not even funny. Like about ten years ago, they got into hard-core Christianity and just flipped their lids. Part of the reason I came out so weird and extreme is a reaction to them. I got involved in Satanism, drugs, and every vile act possible in high school. Gee, how many Commandments can I break? That sort of thing. I've done most of them as it is. I'm doing pretty good. I think I've only got two, three left to break.

I remember one time I brought home a skinhead girlfriend. She had a nose ring. She had this leather miniskirt, fishnets, and big steel-toe combat boots. I was totally enamored of the concept of having this woman that scared my parents. Pissing off my parents was totally a kind of a pleasure. I do enjoy offending people. Just because most people bug me so much.

I like to paraphrase that toothpaste commercial: I'm looking for a whiter, brighter future.

Edwin had glasses and he was nicely dressed. He wasn't like a home-boy or like someone hanging out on the street. I think he was the kind of person who always wanted to look his best. He wanted to make a good impression on people.

We met Edwin at Miomonides Hospital. He was from a group called FACES, which is like an acting group for kids who don't have anything else to do except hang out on the street.

There wasn't really a place to do the interview, so we had to go to the stairwell. I was scared that I would have to ask all these questions and that I wouldn't know what to say, because I've never really had an experience with violence.

But then I didn't have to say anything. He talked for hours and all I did was nod my head. It seemed like he really wanted an outside person to talk to because I wasn't going to judge him about anything. I wasn't going to be like, Well, gee, you're a wimp because you don't fight.

He was like, Well, I don't fight. I don't believe in fighting, whatever. And I could be like, Oh, that's cool. It was someone who wasn't involved in the stuff he had seen around him ever since he was little.

He was very insecure about some things. He felt out of place, I think, because he wasn't involved in violence and stuff like that. And they would tease him because he was short and they would tease him because he was Hispanic. So I think that's what it was.

I don't think he wanted pity at all. He did talk about having low self-esteem. I think he figured it out for himself because he felt so bad. He went through this period of his life where he didn't think he was good at all and he just had no motivation to do anything because he didn't think he was worthy of anything because of what people had said. It was a big thing he had to get over.

I think he did kind of get over it because he does have motivation now. He's going to college and stuff like that.

It was like his overcoming the fact that he was different from other people, like he wouldn't join in racist things. So at first he felt out of place and they would tease him about it, but gradually he came to realize he shouldn't feel stupid about having good ideas. He should be proud.

Cat Deakins, 14, Editor

I was born in Ecuador and I got to Brooklyn when I was four months old. My mother was always tough. She had to be my mother and my father at the same time, even though I had my dad, he would call every day, but still it wasn't the same, it wasn't the same at all.

My mom would wake up at five o'clock in the morning if I was sick or my brother was sick. She would take us in little coats, and she didn't know much English at all, but somehow she would get us to the hospital, all covered up and everything. Sometimes my mom thinks I don't care about her or anything. Like we have arguments, and she thinks that I forget those times, but I don't forget those moments. Somehow, someday, I will pay, repay her back.

I will pay her back because now I'm very glad that I didn't live in the streets. That's good. I didn't hang out a lot, I wasn't with the worst crowds at all. I knew a lot of them, but I didn't get involved with them. I never smoked pot, I never did any drugs at all. I don't drink. But some people, that's their life.

Sometimes, when I was little, there used to be moments when I used to feel ugly, you know, like there's nothing left, that everything you did it's like not even worth it, and you walk around like you don't know where you're going, you don't know why you're doing it, people call you stupid or ugly or fat or other names that mean people call and it hurts. People don't think that it hurts, but after a while, it hurts and you start believing it. And sometimes, I still got that, that self-esteem—it still bothers me a lot, some stuff. But you get over it.

Sometimes, still, when I wake up in the morning, I don't feel like doing anything. I'm ugly. I'm this, I'm that. I don't got any nice clothes. My friends don't like me. Blah, blah, blah, but you get out of it after a while. Some people, though, don't get out of it, they try to commit suicide, and if they've been hearing stories from everybody, what do you tell them? Tell them the same speech everybody else have gave them?

No, I think you have to push, you push, you grab them from the hand, you grab, you hold them, and you say, Look, I understand. You hug them. They might not want a hug, but I bet you if you give them a hug, if you won't let go, I bet you they'll hug you back.

The thing that bothers me most now is racism. You know I am Hispanic. Sometimes I'm walking by and I hear, Hey, Spic, what yo doing here? Or, Hey, goya, we don't want your kind here. And I wonder about that because I'm not embarrassed to be Hispanic. That's definite. I don't mind being Hispanic, but why do people have to stick it in your face? I never understood that. I mean, I don't step on people's feet. I have to walk down the street. Why can't I walk down the street without people saying stuff about me like that? Why is that? I never understood that.

I like to write poems. Every time I have a problem, or feelings, I write it. I was coming back from Brooklyn College and the bus passed right by a Chinese store where they were having problems, and as I watched, I wrote, RACISM IS DUMB.

Sometimes when I am walking down the street and there are old ladies and old men looking scared, like checking their wallets, it bothers me 'cause I never stole anything in my whole life. Never. And I'm not planning to.

There's no reason for me to steal, so why these people, why are they covering, they're looking and expecting you to steal something? If you're behind them, walking behind them, they get nervous if they turn and you turn. Why do they say your kind is this and your kind is that? Your kind get pregnant all the time. Your kind dealing drugs all the time. What's my kind? I'm Hispanic. Are you talking about Hispanics? You're not talking about me. There are plenty of people I know who don't use drugs and they're Hispanic, too. Are we not considered Hispanics also?

Maybe my way of thinking is wrong and I'm the only one left in this world thinking about this. I hope not. But sometimes you just wonder, Am I wrong because I look like this? Because I'm Hispanic?

And then there's some people who make it worse by saying we have to have a quota. At least ten percent black people have to be hired, and five percent of these Hispanic people. So then people say we're going to hire any Spanish person, it doesn't matter what kind of background, because we have to. Why can't we get hired because of experience, instead of just because I'm Spanish I'm gonna get hired? It's not fair. 'Cause you have to be hired by law, not because you're good.

I don't want to be wasting my time in school for four years because I'm Spanish and if I want I can not even go to school and just apply for every job. You need Spanish? I'm perfect. I'm Spanish. I'll just sit at a desk and you just give me a check. That's what it means. I want to be going to four years of college and then I want to be hired because I have experience and I'm good at something. Hopefully, I'm good and people like me because I'm good, not because I'm Spanish.

Yesterday I heard that President Bush is thinking about hiring a Hispanic as a Supreme Court justice, and I thought that's great because not too many Spanish people are up there in the political world. If that happens, maybe I could help other Spanish people say, Look, look at that guy, you could be like him if you work hard and go to school, not drop out, not live on welfare.

Welfare's not what we're here for. We're here to at least do something. Good mostly. I want to do something good.

But there are a lot of people out there who make noise, a whole group of Spanish guys who make noise and people get scared and I don't blame them. I don't understand why they have to hurt somebody. I don't want to hurt somebody. I don't want to go out, look at a girl, and say, She's hot and we're gonna have her, whether she like it or not. That's not fair. When that Central Park thing happened, I was disgusted. I was so embarrassed. I'm glad I don't know none of them, thank God.

I don't know what we can do about violence. I just wish that we don't fight so much with each other. Instead of fighting, I hope we could just build something. Instead of using your hands to fight, why don't we use them to build something? It just seems this world is getting worse and worse every day.

Why can't we love each other? I don't understand, just because we look different, we're different sex, so what? I wish that it could become a nonviolent world, so we could sit back, me and you, and we're no longer into fighting and now people are growing flowers outside, able to leave their doors open. I hope it gets better, 'cause if it gets worse, there isn't going to be nobody left.

Randy and Michelle are two Children's Express editors. Here, they describe their experiences with racism.

RANDY, 18, AND MICHELLE, 19, INDIANAPOLIS

MICHELLE: Have you ever got hassled by the police?

RANDY: Yeah, several times. It makes me feel sad. You ask, What have we done? I've never been locked up, never been in trouble with the law, nothing like that. What have I done to be harassed by the police?

MICHELLE: You're black, that's it, that's all.

RANDY: It's not my fault that I'm black. I'm proud that I'm black. It's not like I walked up to God and said, Make me black.

MICHELLE: I'm glad I'm black.

RANDY: I'm glad I'm black, too, but it's not my fault. And the police treat you like, well, you can't walk the street without police officers looking at you, stopping, turning around, following you.

MICHELLE: Do you think, subconsciously, that society is telling black men that you're a criminal so why not be one?

RANDY: Well, it turns you against a lot of people. Even though I have white friends that aren't like that at all, it makes you wonder. It turns you around. It's turned a lot of people. I'm not saying that it's made me rough, but it's had me thinking hard a lot of times.

One time I was standing on the corner and cops just rolled up, about eight of them, and they pinned me up against the wall, me and my cousin. They told us they were going to kill us because this one police officer's wife said we had jumped on her

125

car, threatened to kill her, called her this and that. Her husband stuffed the nightstick up to our necks. It was all up in my throat and I couldn't breathe.

MICHELLE: What was going through your mind?

RANDY: I was mad. You know how you feel when your parents tell you you've done something that you know you haven't done? You're like, I didn't do that, and your parents are like, I know you did.

MICHELLE: You're mad because you can't fight back but you want to.

RANDY: I knew I hadn't done anything, but this officer and his friends were telling me, You've done it, and there was nothing I could do. They had the guns, they had the sticks, they had the manpower. It was just little old me, a piddly little thing, versus what they had. So it's sad that black males are depicted in society as criminals. It deters some of them from going after what they want to get. People have this stereotype of a big, black male, just looking for trouble. Any time anyone sees a big, black male coming towards them, they get scared. I even get scared.

MICHELLE: Me too, and I wish I wouldn't. It's weird how we've been socialized.

RANDY: We've been programmed.

MICHELLE: Yes, we have. But working on this book is helping to deprogram.

HOMOPHOBIA

In a lot of ways, when I was younger, I was afraid of violence and I still am when I see it. I freeze. But if I'm involved in it, I'll go for it, as violent and bloody as I can get.

JOSÉ, 20

I'm not actively going out there and killing heterosexuals, but I'm also not going to stand there and take it.

CHARLES, 18

We met José through the Berkeley Gay Youth Help Program. He was medium height, had black hair and a black goatee. He was dressed in bright-colored clothes, kind of flashy. He was the kind of person who seems confident in the way that he is.

I had a lot of respect for José because he really wants to educate people, to make them realize that homosexuals are people, too. Just because they have different sexual preferences doesn't make them non-humans.

That's the way he wants to live his life and that's the way he's going to, just for himself. He has problems with his parents because they're not understanding about the way that he is.

Shane Tilston, 17, Editor

JOSÉ, 20, BERKELEY

My name is Xavier . . . Javier . . . José . . . accent on the e, and I prefer Xavier to be spelled with an X, so it's Xavier, thank you. I live in Berkeley, California and I was raised near here. My mother and my father were married for convenient reasons. He was an illegal alien and so they married just so that he could get his green card and stay in the United States.

Out of that marriage of convenience my sister and I were born, but there really wasn't too much love or commitment between my parents. They each had their own separate boyfriends and girlfriends. They would constantly get mad at each other and fight a lot and really did a lot of bodily damage to each other.

I remember one night, when I was four years old, my father came home very drunk, very sloshed, and he passed out in the middle of the living-room floor. My mother grabbed him by his ankles and just drug him around the house and down the stairs so he could smack his head on the stairs. He couldn't do anything about it because he was so wasted. The next day, my father grabbed a glass ashtray and smashed her in the jaw with it. They separated when I was five.

Since then I haven't really been a part of my father's life

much. Every now and again I'll come back into it. I told him that I was gay last Christmas. I spoke Spanish to him, which is something I usually don't do. I told him in Spanish, Dad, I'm gay. And he didn't believe me. He kept asking me, No, you're not gay. No, you're not. I'm like, Yeah, I am. I was shaking so bad and it was so weird, 'cause at the same time when I was talking to him about this, the song by the Temptations, "Daddy's Home," was playing in the background. I just thought it was really kind of poetic. And he was very upset.

The next day we were walking in the park and he was asking me to explain it to him, and he got really upset and started beating up a soccer ball and sort of like walked off. He was refusing to understand it, so the last I really spoke to him was, Well, maybe I should just go home. And he said, Yeah, maybe you should. And so he took me to the train station and I got the train back home.

In a way it made me feel bad because I knew the main reason why I told him that I was gay was to get back at him. I was really hurt a lot, you know, seeing him and my mother fight all the time, and seeing them break up. I mean, I didn't care much at all for my mother, and my father was like the world to me, and so when he left it was really devastating for me. But I didn't tell anyone about it. I told him I was gay just to get back at him. Now I feel really awful. I feel really bad that I would willfully hurt someone that much.

You know, it's funny, but I think I would make a great father. Because I thought my father was a really great father. I mean, I only have feelings and memories and images to go on, but I remember whenever I'd see him, the only thing I wanted to do was like run up and jump up in his arms. I wouldn't see him that often, only nights and on weekends. And even though he was dog-ass tired, and pissed off and cranky, he would still have time for his kids. He would still have time to spend with me—to raise me until I was five.

But then he left and I'm really bitter because I loved him a lot. He chose to leave and didn't take me. He left me with this woman that I really didn't like too much. I mean she was my mother and I loved her a lot, but she would not have been my choice as a parent.

My mother went through this severe I-hate-men thing. It was really, really bad. If she had any opportunity to cut any man down for any reason, she would take it. I would be like laying down resting my head in her lap or something and she would look down and say, You know the only reason why I love you is because you're my son. Things like that would really make me feel very bitter.

It's sort of weird with my father, too. He came out and took me out to lunch and kept asking, Is there anything I can do for you? Can I send you to a doctor? Can I give you medication? Is there anything I can do? Maybe you can go live with your brother and watch him and his wife and maybe it'll rub off on you. And I was trying to explain to him it's not a psychological problem, it's not a physical condition, it's not a disease, it's not a sociology thing, you don't pick it up through osmosis, because before I discovered the gay community I thought I was straight and then I discovered that I was gay. I didn't discover that I was straight. You understand? So being around straights wouldn't have helped me at all. Jerks!

Until I was in junior high school I didn't have any male friends. All of my friends were girls. I would just hang out with them and play with their Barbies and stuffed animals and things like that because that's what I thought was fun. I didn't like playing baseball or football or dirt bikes. It just didn't interest me.

Later on, when I was first coming up, I was flaming. I was a flaming homosexual. I was on fire. Other people looked at me and gave me shit for it. And I thought about it and decided that's really kind of showy and very arrogant. It really wasn't me. I think that more than anything else, what pisses a lot of straight people off about gay people is their arrogance. And being flaming. I don't think it's really necessary. So I sort of stopped and now I feel very turned off by flaming men.

When I was at my most flaming, I had this Mohawk, it was like three inches thick and the bangs were down to my collarbone and the back was down to the middle of my back and it was shaved completely on the sides. This is when I was in high school. It was big and fluffy and I would wear lots of thick black eyeliner and brown wool tuxedos with combat boots. This was the type of school where everyone was either wearing things from the Gap or Miller's Outpost or jeans and a T-shirt. For the most part they would just look at me and every now and again I'd get a heartfelt "Freak!"

In a way it felt good. I liked being different. I liked being so different from these people that I would do just about anything to the extreme so I could not be associated with them. I didn't want them to associate with me because I didn't like them. I thought they were phony and one thing I can't stand is phony people.

So I figured if I go to the extreme for myself, then those people who would just be judgmental on the way I look would not approach me. And those who didn't care about the way I looked and wanted to know the person that I am would approach me. And those are the people I wanted to deal with.

Rejection stuff gives me a really bad, explosive temper at times, but I'm usually very good at keeping it in control. If I get like really pissed to the point where I'm going to hurt someone, I remove myself from the situation and I'll jump up and down, holler up and down and in circles and punch my fists and maybe scream at the top of my lungs, because I just want to haul off and pop someone who really needs it.

I think it carries over into the connections, the emotional connections that I've had. Because I'll start like a playful sort of type violence, but then it will sort of like escalate. It'll start off with wrestling or something like that and then it'll just get a little bit more intense, a little bit more aggressive, and I feel myself really enjoying it, really wanting it to get big and confrontational, and then I'll stop myself from it.

In a lot of ways, when I was younger, I was afraid of violence and I still am when I see it. I freeze. But if I'm involved in it, I'll go for it, as violent and bloody as I can get.

I think a lot of it is animalistic. But maybe that's just me rationalizing it. I feel a lot of it being fueled by rage. And having no control over the situations that were going on when I was younger. Here I am, in the prime of my life feeling very powerful and feeling the ability to like thrash someone. And a lot of times I just want to. Just to know what it feels like. And it's really kind of scary to me. 'Cause it feels really primal, and I feel like I have no control over it. I just want to know what it feels like.

I've really lost a lot of hope for a lot of people, mostly because of the violence and how violent people can be. It makes me think that there's no romance and no love left in the world, because everyone is coming from a violent sort of background and it's going to stop everyone from completely giving to other people.

I want to be able to find a person that not only can I talk with, but I can joke with and be romantic with, be silly, be a freak. You know, be whatever. Be someone that I could feel comfortable raising a child with. Because that's what I want to do. I want to raise a child. I want a white picket fence. I want a little house in the suburbs. I want him to go to work and I want to clean the house. I'm so domestic. Don't worry, I'll get over it. Someday. Not soon, I hope. It's my life-long dream. God, I sound so Alice Fay.

I think a lot and I analyze things a lot, and I write, I write constantly. I wonder if my logs are ever found people are going to read them and go, God! This guy was depressed all the time. He was doing nothing but bitching in these pages. And sometimes I feel that's all I'm ever doing, but I don't know, it's my way of getting out what I feel. Because it's not all bad. There's a lot of romance in my pages. There's a lot of happiness. A lot of joy, too.

Charles was happy to do an interview. He was pretty thin, wore wire-rimmed round glasses, and had a shaved head. He wore a T-shirt and a pair of jeans.

The way it happened to him when he came out, he wasn't able even to explain it to his parents, his brother did. And his religion failed him, too. He is Jewish and his rabbi excommunicated him. So the option he chose was to say, Well, this is what I am, everyone's going to know it, and I'm going to be proud of it, no matter what. Sort of fight the system and don't hide from it. Be blatant about it, let everyone know and take what they're going to give, which he's been taking a lot of.

It was kind of scary. When you read his story, you see the kinds of things he has to go through, just in day-to-day life. It reminds you of the stuff you hear about happening in the South against blacks, the way they'd basically live in fear because there was so much that could happen to them. It reminds me of that. It's sort of scary how there's that kind of stuff going on nowadays.

I'm sure, when he first started realizing that he was homosexual, there was a lot of confusion, feeling "I'm not like my friends" kind of thing. There was no one really there, no one to support him at all. He couldn't turn to his family. His own brother betrayed him to his parents. He couldn't turn to religion. He hadn't even any support from his friends at school. Everyone was just afraid of him when he came out.

I could understand how he just got angry at it all and said, Well, if you're not going to help me, then I'm just going to do it by myself and screw you all. He is very angry.

Shane Tilston, 17, Editor

CHARLES, 18, BERKELEY

I'm a student at Berkeley. My major is English. My minor is Women's Studies. I just completed my freshman year.

I went to a small, fascist, conservative prep school in Brooklyn and I was the first "out" person to make it to graduation. I also was the first person in my grade to get an earring. When I started wearing it around, the head of the high school came to me and said, Charlie, either stop wearing the earring or we're going to make earrings illegal next year and that will mean nobody can wear an earring. So I just kept wearing an earring.

I really was kind of quiet and when I came out, all of a sudden, I blossomed. I was much more social, 'cause when you come out, you need friends desperately and you need people who are in common with you. I used to hang out with thirteen-year-old drag queens who'd imitate Diana Ross extremely well. My energy was not really accepted in the school, so I did not spend much time whatsoever there.

I've always been progressive. I think it comes from experience. When I was in New York, I personally had it easy. I was outed to my parents, out of the closet, by my brother. I was out of the house for three days and my sister flew in to rescue me.

When I came out in high school, people were afraid of me, afraid to be seen with me. But once I told my parents, I could do anything, and I did. When you come out in high school, the first thing that happens is the gay teachers treat you like total shit. They make life hard for you because they're afraid of being ferreted out of the closet. So they've got to appear to be three times as much of an asshole as everybody else so they can preserve their little jobs.

I got out here and I was gay-bashed in the dormitories by all these football players. I would get death threats on my door. I would get things like "Die, faggot" or "All you faggots should burn in hell and be hung at the stake" and everything. And there was this clique of "out" gay people, and linemen on the football team would threaten to break jaws and it was really very hellish.

The university totally does not back you up whatsoever. I mean they don't take it seriously. I shocked them by putting on this homophobia forum, which got people to talk about their experiences of homophobia. The actual homophobes showed up and said things like, I've bashed gays before and I would do it again. . . . When you look at us you are violating our personal space, which is not okay to do to men, therefore we have a right to fuck you up and you should expect it. Some of the things they said were really horrendous. It was a nightmare.

I invited cops from East Bay to the forum for protection because we didn't feel quite safe and after the forum we had to be escorted home. And then there were people outside my door and window talking and the cops came to chase them away. It was just a really scary experience, and so I'm fairly down on the politically correct college community out here.

I've been working in the dormitory for the summer and the stuff I get at work is like, Work it, bitch. And I get "faggot" screamed at me all the time when my back is turned. Really brave people! I get whistled at and get "You could be my girl-friend." That's at work.

If I'm in a really dangerous situation, I go by instinct and I get out of there. Like I don't go near frat row at night. I don't get in cabs right after getting out of bars and clubs, I always walk away and hail one down. That's a problem because gay men get in cabs and get taken on wild rides and get harassed and mugged by cab drivers who are waiting out in front of gay bars.

I do my little stuff against it, like I'm beginning to volunteer for Community Night Against Violence. I'm going to go into high schools and basically say, Look, you can't gay-bash any-more because some gay men may turn you around and clean your clock, fuck you up, like me. That's what I want to do, but I'm going to have to be trained to be nice and polite, which I am going to hate, but I'll do my best.

I mean, most of these people haven't gone through the ex-perience. I came out in the dormitories and nobody talked to me and none of my friends were in the dormitories and still none of them are because nobody talks to you except other gay people who get up the courage to say hello.

Issues of homophobia never really get addressed. They are just not seen as important or as bad as racism or sexism or things like that. It's frustrating.

The violence against us is the hardest part. One time in New York I was held up at gunpoint on Christopher Street. This guy pointed a gun at me and said, Fag, give me your money. And then the football team would physically threaten me and they tried to beat one of my friends with a chair. He was straight, but they thought he was gay.

But, you know, you get used to it. I think a lot of racial harassment goes unreported because people just get used to it, you get very used to it. And either you combat it or it doesn't affect your general life 'cause no matter what you do, the levels don't decrease.

I get pissed, though, I mean I get pissed. I would be lying if I didn't say I get angry. Every now and then I have attacks of the gas-pedal syndrome—I'll be out in my car and a man will cross in front of me and I'll just want to step on the gas pedal and smash him.

Basically, now, my family is my gay friends, my gay and straight friends who deal with me. They offer me strength and support and I support them, too. When one of my lesbian friends was raped in an alley last semester, we came together for her and I was so impressed with that. I said, Wow. And then there have been times when I have been harassed and my friends have come together for me and supported me. So I sort of like them better than my biological family.

Except for my sister. She's awesome. All her friends are gay. She's a fag hag. She is bisexual, but nobody knows that. She is wonderful and I love her totally. We totally get along and we've got so much in common. She's the only member of my biological family that I can truly say is a friend.

My parents are just weird. They're nice, but they are my parents and they don't deserve much more. My brother is an uptight, intellectual Republican who I absolutely despise. I'm not really close with any of my extended family, either, and I don't care. As a matter of fact, whenever I meet them I try to make them as uncomfortable as possible because they are orthodox Jewish and they hate me.

Just recently, for the first time, I've gotten shit for being Jewish at work. And it is such a breather! It's like, Wow, this is such a relief. For once, it's nonhomophobic shit. But it's funny, too, because I haven't really identified as being Jewish since when I came out. I basically got told I was no longer a Jew by a rabbi. So I thought, You mean it? I'm free?! I was really kind of happy to be excommunicated by the Jewish community of New York. That is definitely not my scene.

I'm not giving up on the violence and stuff. I'm doing my volunteer work, but I think it's a serious problem that people put people who are different down. In some cultures, people who are different are sacred. I mean, people should be accepted as other and their right not to assimilate and not be looked down upon should be accepted on their terms, not on the majority's terms.

But no matter what you do, our society says, Fuck the few. So what you have to do is fuck back. You do volunteer work. You do self-defense. You give yourself a reputation not to be messed with by going after one of them and beating the shit out of them, something like that you have to do.

America just better learn to deal with it because we're here. And they better watch out because people are just going to fuck back. I mean, the more oppressive society gets and the more shit people take, the more people give shit back and militant they become. So if you are complaining about any militancy or you complained about being alienated by minorities, maybe you should look at what's being done to the minorities and deal with that.

I mean, it may not be you personally, but it could be your friends and it's everybody's responsibility that there is violence. If they deny responsibility, then they're twice as guilty.

I'm not actively going out there and killing heterosexuals, but I'm also not going to stand there and take it. If I can do something, I will do something and that's that. I'm not going to sit there and play Mahatma Gandhi or Martin Luther King. There are better people to do that role than me. I just want to get out of there alive.

We visited the Hedrick-Martin Institute in New York, a drop-in counseling and resource center for young lesbians and gay men. We spoke with Michelle, who is agonizing about her sexual orientation.

Emily Ashton, 16
Omri Elisha, 17
Editors

MICHELLE, 18, NEW YORK CITY

I cut my hair in my freshman year of high school. Through-out that whole year, I got beat up and guys tried to rape me in the back of my school. People use to call me names and say, Look at that dyke walking down the street. That was hard, but I think the internal stuff was harder.

I pretty much hated myself for a long time without really knowing why. Up to this day, until this year, I've had a very difficult time saying the word *lesbian*. I used to have to look in the mirror and say, I am a lesbian. Yes, I am a lesbian, I really am. I would say it over and over a million times, but as I said it that person in the mirror wasn't me. I was talking to somebody else and that was fine. I couldn't say it to myself and I couldn't recognize it within myself, even though I knew what I felt and what I wanted to do.

Right now the girl that I'm seeing can't come out to her parents, because even when they only thought she was a lesbian, they beat her up with a telephone wire. They forced her to tell me that she hated me and never wanted to see me again. They beat her until she was almost dead and had to go to the hospital. Her father wanted her to get inspected by the gynecologist so they could prove that she had been sexually assaulted by me.

5

Tough Guys

I hate niggers and I hate tightwad Jews. I hate people who work in tall buildings and make lots of money and laugh at everybody else who doesn't.

Tod, 22

I guess you could say that I'm violent because I grew up with it. I missed a lot of stuff that I would have appreciated. So now I'm just rude and crude and obnoxious, just like Bart Simpson. I can be a nice enough person if I want to, I suppose. No big deal.

Thai, 18

Tough guys.

Land of Diminishing Dreams . . .

_____

The year is two thousand fifty-four,
The world is full of curses.
People walk the streets no more,
No women carry purses.

The name of the game is survival now—
Safety is far in the past.
Families are huge, with tons of kids
In hopes that one will last.

Drugs are no longer looked down upon,
They are a way of life.
They help us escape the wrenching stress
Of our fast world's endless strife . . .

I wake up now—it was only a dream,
But the message was terribly clear.
We'd better think hard about the future
Before our goals and our dreams disappear.

JESSICA INGLIS, 16

Skinheads.

Tod was from San Francisco. He was very much like the typical stereotype of a skinhead. He wore the uniform: combat boots with white laces, black suspenders, and his flight jacket.

When I started talking with him, he was very two-dimensional in what he believed and the way he spoke. I remember he actually said, What do those blacks want? We gave them the privilege of being our slaves, and stuff like that that's just so blatantly stupid, you can't take it seriously. I had the sense that he didn't really know what he was talking about, like it had sort of gotten drilled into him, or he had grabbed on to something just because his friends were doing it.

I felt a little afraid at some points, just because he was so convinced that what he believed in was right. It was scary knowing that he would actually kill someone because of what he believes. He believed he was superior—just because of the color of his skin—over someone who looked different than he did. The whole way he lived his life around that, just totally believing in it, but not understanding it. Not having any reason at all behind it. It was a pretty short interview because he didn't really have much to say other than I'm better, kill them all.

So I didn't really find out much about him as a person, he was so buried in anger. Even the anger seemed sort of redirected instead of what he really believed. It seemed like there was something else, that this is just sort of the out that he's found, a way to express the anger and be tolerated by his friends. This would be accepted, he decided, so he just jumped in there with both feet.

Shane Tilston, 17, Editor

TOD, 22, SAN FRANCISCO

Well, let's see. I guess you could say my childhood was fucked. I was raised in a suburban home by an alcoholic family. Fucked-up school years. I got my GED in tenth grade, so that tells you how my school was like. I got into fights, doing stupid shit to the teachers. I was basically the class clown. I don't like authority a lot. I have a real problem with authority. So that's basically my childhood in a nutshell, man. It sucked.

My parents were both born in Ireland, and they're typical,

they're not like the religious, sober Irish people. They're the drunk and rowdy Irish people. They constantly beat on each other and beat on me until I learned I could beat back.

Typical Irish-American means violence. A lot of drinking. Meat and potatoes and beer. Lots of potatoes. Violence-prone family is what it was. I don't have any religion. My dad's not anything, either. I think we used to be Protestant, but I'm not sure. I know I got family in the IRA [Irish Republican Army].

I've been living on my own for a while. I moved out of my house when I was sixteen. I was sick of the bullshit. So I got put in jail for a while. I did four years.

Now I'm into the skin scene and basically trying to keep the streets clean. We have a problem. I live up on Cole Street and that's where all the crack niggers hang out. They seem to want to fucking take over the city. They think they can come up here and sell crack on our street, but we've been keeping this street clean for I don't know how many years. Then, all of a sudden, they move in and think they fucking own this place. They're pulling guns on people, robbing people daily. I mean we're no angels, we go out and attack people all the time, but those niggers are up there pulling guns out on people and holding them up at gunpoint.

We've had death threats made at us. Last night, forty or fifty niggers came in here and jumped on four skinheads. Beat up on the skingirls, man. That's the kind of shit that's uncalled for up here, man. We need to take care of that problem. People been saying, Oh yeah, we're going to get it done, we're going to get it done. But it ain't going nowhere. When I came up here, there was no fucking crack dealers on that corner. I live on that street. I have to walk past that every night. I get harassed. I get forty bottles thrown at me. It's pathetic. This street has gone down.

So I beat 'em up, whenever I get the chance. I just get up and sock them. 'Cause, you know, I sell drugs here. I'm going to admit that right now. I sell drugs. I sell pot and I sell doses. That's the way I make my living. I also work at a tattoo shop.

I'm not going to reveal where it is 'cause that would be going too far. These guys come down here, they sell their crack, they make a hell of a lot of money, and they give us a bad name. They come to this part and they start problems with you. It's bullshit. Haight Street used to be a nice place to be and now it's a fucking jungle, just like downtown.

I got involved by choice. I just came down here, saw the scene, the money was good, and I said, Yep. So I'm making cash now, and I'm happy. I have my own place, and that's basically it for me.

I also tax people a lot, I go out and take shit from them. If I see something I want, if I see something that I think somebody doesn't deserve to be wearing, I just take it. I'm a skinhead and my uniform is boots, braces, and a flight jacket. If I see somebody that I think is walking around trying to claim to be something they're not, then I'll tax 'em and take what they have on. Like their flight jacket or their boots. I don't tax my family. I just tax people who are stupid enough to come up to me and fuck with me or walk past me with a sneer on their face. I beat 'em up because I don't like that shit. Half the time I'm drunk anyway, so what the fuck, you know what I mean?

I'm a racist. I'm very racist. I'm Aryan. I'm as fucking Aryan as you can get and I'm proud to be that way. I don't believe in race mixing. I don't believe in interracial relationships. I don't believe that people like that should be on our street. I wouldn't mind them being here if they weren't selling crack to everybody, getting everybody hooked on crack and coming up here and getting us busted for them selling crack. When they come up and sell crack, it gets the cops over there all riled up.

We never had that much attention brought to us before. I mean we can sit down here and sell huge garbage bags of weed and no one would say anything. The cops would leave us alone. This has always been a relaxed place to sell drugs. But these fuckers come up here and sell their crack and pawn their women off on my street. That's not going on. I'm sorry, it just doesn't work that way.

145

My dad's racist, too. He's racist as hell. I picked up these views when I was young. My whole family is Irish. Nobody in my family has married anybody but an Irish person. I might be the first to do that. It depends. I just want me a nice white woman that I can have babies with and fall in love and have a nice house and get a good, hard-working job. Which will probably be owning my own tattoo shop pretty soon.

I plan to stick to my views. I'm not going to change them for nobody no how. To me, a completely white family, that's it. A white United States, a white world would be a nice one. Those guys should feel privileged that we even brought them over here to America, man. We gave them the privilege of being our slaves and now they're taking advantage of it.

I don't think in my life we're going to get rid of all the niggers, but I think we might be able to pull it off one of these days. Mass extermination may be the only way. I hate niggers and I hate tightwad Jews. I hate any corporate tightwad capitalist bastard. I hate people who work in tall buildings and make lots of money and laugh at everybody else who doesn't. So what if you've got a better job than me, does that make you better than me?

I think I'm better than everybody else, but that's just my personal opinion, of course. I just feel I'm better than everybody else. If anybody has a problem with that, well then, we'll fight and see who's better.

You may say that my beliefs are stupid, but I think some other people's beliefs are stupid. I think hippies are dumb, but I hang out with them and I respect them 'cause they're my family up here. This is Haight Street, man, this is supposed to be the land of peace and love and LSD. What happened to fucking peace? I mean there's chaos, violence, and crack right now. It's not peace-loving anymore.

I advocate violence, but on my own terms. When I advocate violence, it's because I feel I want to fight one person. If I go up to a person, I challenge that one person. I don't mob people. I don't like to do that. But if it happens, then it happens. If a mob

146

of people comes on me, then a mob of my friends is going to join in. That's just the way it is.

I don't preach my politics to anybody. If they don't want to hear it, then they can tell me to shut up and go away and I will. Because I believe in freedom of speech, and I believe in freedom of religion, and I believe in freedom of belief. You can believe what you want to, but that doesn't mean that I can't in my own mind hate you for what you believe or the color of your skin.

My parents respect my views, they agree with it. If anybody thinks they're going to be able to stop me from believing that way, then four years in jail didn't stop me from believing it. Jail actually helped me a lot. I joined the Aryan Brotherhood there and I stuck with them, you know.

I'm getting my shit together now, but my life until now has been basically screwed. I'm trying to be working class, I got an apartment, I've got a good job, and another good job drug dealing. That's my life, man. That's basically all there is to it, that's all she wrote on me, man. I have a very boring life.

Thai was really scary. He had really long hair—I think it was purple—and he was kind of dirty. He had these big tattoos. At first he wasn't interested in talking to us, but then when we said it was going to be in a book, he was interested.

We sat on a bench by the fountain in Washington Square Park and as the conversation went on his friends sort of gathered around us and he seemed to be showing off to them. He was very frightening and said some really extreme things, but I think he just wanted to scare us, or at least get a reaction out of us. I think he was lying half of the time. I couldn't believe that he was so calmly saying the things he said, like putting a power drill through some guy's shoulder. I think he must have been under the influence of something. He didn't seem to be all there.

Thai was the one person in this whole book who scared me the most and I honestly hope that I never see him again. With people like him running around in our society, lots of people are going to get hurt.

Sarah Young, 16, Editor

THAI, 18, NEW YORK CITY

My name is Thai and I'm known as the resident maniac of Washington Square Park. I climb up in trees, jump down on tourists, stuff like that. I'm bored, mostly. I like to shake people up.

I like to have fun with people, you know? Like I'll walk up to a small dog owner, point at the dog, and shout, *Lunge!* The owner will look at me like I'm insane and start moving quickly for the nearest exit, taking their dog with them. I'll borrow a kid's water gun and start running around the park squirting people who look like they don't want to be squirted. I'm just a practical joker. I like having fun with people.

When I'm not in the park, I go uptown and see *Rocky Horror Picture Show*. Haven't missed a show yet, four years straight.

I live on the East Side, or at least my parents do. Most of the time I'm either grounded or I'm kicked out of the house. Hey, fuck it, I say. When I'm kicked out, I just kick the door in, take what I want to, lock the door so nobody can get in, and then go to a friend's house for a couple of weeks. My parents are schizophrenic, or at least I think so. So do some of my friends who know them. Then again, everybody's parents are schizophrenic at one point or another.

My parents are really weird. They chew you out about your friends or what time you stay out till, stuff like that. When my stepdad gets on one of his kicks, he'll start ragging out some of my friends. He did that last week, threw a punch at me, broke his wrist, and walked out of the house, no big deal. I went home Friday to get changed up for *Rocky*. I wear all black and put Noxzema on my face really thick to look like a vampire, put in my pointed teeth, stuff like that.

I used to go to a private school out on Long Island, but I got into a little problem out there. Somebody tried to pull a gun on me, but I got to mine first and I shot him in the knee. No big deal. He tried it again six months later. That time he came out a little worse for wear. I shot him through his shoulder, the shoulder he was shooting with. I don't think he'll be trying to pull guns out on anybody anymore.

I got rid of all my guns before I went to prison. I was accused of doing a bank robbery. *Accused*, but nobody could prove a fucking thing and no, I did not do it. I got railroaded in, just did eighteen months on a one and a half to four and a half. I didn't take the trial. I copped out 'cause my lawyer told me that was the lowest offer I was going to ever get, so I took it. Did eighteen months. No big deal.

Sometimes I feel like turning into a cop killer, sometimes I don't. Sometimes I feel like going hunting for the judge that railroaded me. But I know if I'm caught I'll do either life plus or twenty-five to life. And I just don't feel like going to prison for that long.

Prison's like any other place you go to, except it's got bars and you can't leave when you want to. A couple of guys tried to slice me, so I sliced them back. Hit one guy in the jaw with a steel mop ringer. He's probably still drinking from a straw. Those guys are a joke.

One time I put a power drill through somebody's joints. Put it through his shoulder joints and I put it through his knees. And then I just left him there. He did some things that I didn't appreciate to a friend of mine. He hasn't been back. I'm looking forward to the time he does come back. Then we're going to have fun.

I guess you could say that I'm violent because I grew up with it. I missed a lot of stuff that I would have appreciated. So now I'm just rude and crude and obnoxious, just like Bart Simpson. I can be a nice enough person if I want to, I suppose. No big deal.

We met Marshall at Little Five Points, an open-air shopping mall in Atlanta. It's where the guys who were stoned and a lot of weird people go, a lot of people with spikes on their heads. A lot of runaways, too. That's where they go to relax, I guess, and get drugs.

Marshall was standing against a pole, waiting for his contact to buy LSD. He looked like the type who would have a lot of problems. He may have had a little marijuana or something, but he did a real good ass-kicking interview, I think, because I wanted to cry myself.

He had long blond hair. He was thin. He wore white jeans shorts, a T-shirt, and no shoes. His hair was a mess. At first he didn't want to be interviewed, but once we started talking to him, he really opened up to us. We could see the sadness in his face when he told us about finding his mother dead and never getting to tell her he loved her. It seemed as though he was doing drugs because he wanted to forget his problems and his pain. He had so much guilt and really seemed to hate himself. I saw it in his face. He just wanted to die right there.

I told him there were plenty of kids in my neighborhood in Brooklyn who were much more messed up than him, and they got help and are doing okay now.

I hope everything is going all right with him now. I hope he got help.

Eric Zamora, 16, Editor
with Rolando Liriano, 16, Editor

MARSHALL, 21, ATLANTA

CE: What was your childhood like?

MARSHALL: My childhood really sucked, man. My dad was an outlaw biker. He was never around and he ended up shooting a copper, so he spent pretty much all of my childhood in prison. My mom pretty much raised me and my two brothers and then she married this asshole and like gave us away to other people who adopted us because she didn't want us no more. But it was our fault, I guess, because we used to hassle her, we used to go out and stay gone for a while. So she just ended up giving us away. She chose her new husband over us.

151

She gave us away to this fat person. Her name was Fat Thelma. She was a big old bat, a ton of lard. I swear to God, man, she sucked. Then finally, after four or five years, we ended up getting back with our mother.

And about a month after I got back with my mother, she died. She had a heart attack and me and my little brother found her. My older brother was in the army at the time. We found her dead right there on her bed. That was fucked up, man. I mean, you look at somebody, they're all blue in the face, especially your mother, you know what I mean?

But there's nothing I can do about it now because she's dead. I don't really care, you know. Fuck it. I mean, there was nothing I can do. Once somebody's dead, they're dead.

After that I went back to live with the fat people and they just treated me like shit. So I just started rebelling and stuff. I started shaving my head into a Mohawk. I just wanted to tell society to fuck off, you know, that it wasn't fair. And it still isn't fair. I got a ripped life, man. I got ripped off.

CE: You still have the chance to change it, you know.

MARSHALL: No, man, I'm just too fucked up in the brain. I am.

CE: No you're not, I perceive that you could change. I'm serious, brother. Around my way a lot of people changed. They were like you, all sick in the head, but they changed and they went back to school and now they're like, Wow, did I really do it? They went to school and they got their lives straight. It's like some miracle, you know, so I think you could still do it.

MARSHALL: Well, let's see, how old are you? Fifteen years old?

CE: I'm sixteen.

MARSHALL: You're sixteen. I'm twenty-one, bro.

CE: It doesn't matter. I mean, my aunt, she's Spanish and she doesn't understand a bit of English, but she's going to school because she wants to make a living, and she's thirty-nine or forty. So you could change, man. You could still change. Tell me about your school.

MARSHALL: I dropped out in eighth grade. Well, actually, I didn't drop out, I got kicked out. Some guy kicked my ass in the cafeteria, in front of all these people, and I was like a little troublemaker in the school anyhow, you know. So this guy kicked my ass in the cafeteria and the next day I came there with a .25 automatic fixing to kill him. And they caught me with the gun and they put me in this alternative school, which is in Jacksonville. So I was there, selling drugs and selling pot and smoking, and then they took me out of there, they kicked me out of there and put me in the last school that you can go to. That one's called Johnny Ford. And after that, I just dropped out.

I've mostly been in trouble with the law. Burglary, selling drugs, that's about it, mainly. When I was a little kid, about your all's age, I was a little fuckin' bugger, man. I used to break into cars and schools and churches and houses and everything.

CE: How did you feel about all that?

MARSHALL: When I was doing it? I didn't care, man. I just wanted to do it and plus I needed the money.

CE: Did you get into a lot of fights?

MARSHALL: No, not really. I was mostly drunk. I don't like to fight. I just hate my life. I think it sucks, you know? It just really sucks, man. Fuck people in general, man. Everybody, everybody sucks, man. People just ain't no good, man. They not. Uh-uh.

CE: There are some people who are good, and there are some people who are assholes.

MARSHALL: There are good people, I suppose, but the majority are assholes. I just want to grow pot, man, that's all I want to do.

153

CE: Are you respected here? Are you well known to everybody?

MARSHALL: No, because I don't have nobody that cares about me. Nobody cares for me, man, nobody at all.

CE: I think you could still help yourself, man. You should get some help, you know what I'm saying?

MARSHALL: What kind of help do you think I should get, man?

CE: You should get into a club, or a rehab, or something like that.

MARSHALL: Fuck the rehabs, man. That won't do shit. I'll just deal with it the best I can. That's the only way I know how to do.

CE: If you ever had any kids, would you raise them differently than your parents raised you?

MARSHALL: Yeah, I would. I'd raise them like I would want to be raised, you know? I would just let them do whatever they wanted to. I wouldn't let them go out and get in trouble with the law, but I wouldn't hit 'em or anything like that, either. I think that's pretty much what made me rebel so much. That's why I'm fucked up, man.

CE: Don't say that. You can still get help. I'm telling you, I know it. I know you could get help.

MARSHALL: I probably could, man, but it just takes too much time and I don't have too much time, you know. I'm not going to live too much longer, man. I'm not, and I don't really give a fuck whether I live or die. I would much rather be dead, you know. 'Cause when I leave here, my existence on this Earth will have no meaning anyway. Not when I'm dead, it won't. It will have no meaning. It just won't.

CE: I don't know, but something's telling me that I still think you could change. Look, I come from New York, man, I came all the way down here to hear your story and I'm saying I know you could change.

MARSHALL: Yeah, that's true, man.

CE: You know, around my way there's a lot of people that take crack, take cocaine, dope, everything in the book—the needle, everything. And they change, they've changed. They used to say the same shit you're saying right now. And then, it's like all of a sudden, I see them and they're like a whole new person and their life is like marvelous, man. I know you could change.

MARSHALL: That's cool, man.

CE: You know, I think you should try to get some help.

MARSHALL: I should, man.

CE: You should.

MARSHALL: I should, man, but I don't really think nobody can help me because I've been doing what I've been doing for just too long. I've been doing it for at least four or five years and I don't think nobody can help me. Besides that, I don't really want to be helped. I kind of like my life. As far as it is right now, if I was to die tomorrow, it would do me just fine. Though I have been kind of good lately. I have been a good boy. That's what my girlfriend calls me.

CE: Aren't you afraid to lose your girlfriend?

MARSHALL: Kind of. Yeah, I am, really. But I don't think it matters much, really, because people don't care about me, man. People don't care.

155

CE: But I care, and I think you can get help. You've already helped yourself a lot. You said you used to be a crack addict and now you're not. And you did it by yourself. You quit by yourself, which is more than most people can do.

MARSHALL: I don't know much about myself. I just know that I suck, that I don't belong here, man, I just belong somewhere else. I wish I was a cat, man, you know? I wish I was a cat or a dog or something like that. Why do I have to be a human? I want to be something else, man.

CE: Do you believe in God?

MARSHALL: No, man, I don't believe in God. Fuck all that shit, man. Can you prove it?

CE: No, I cannot prove it. Nobody can prove it.

MARSHALL: It's just a bunch of bullshit, man. Somebody was smoking pot and wrote the Bible, that's all it was. Maybe Jesus did exist at one time and maybe he did get hung up on that cross, but until I die, I don't want to believe in it. Even when I die, I still don't want to believe in it because it's a bunch of bullshit. That's all it is. Just something to give people, something to give people hope when they die. That's all it is, man.

CE: If you want to, you can let out all your anger right now, bro, right now into this mike, just say what you really feel.

MARSHALL: I loved my mother, man. I did. And I miss her. I just loved my mother, man. That's all I have to say.

6

Lock 'Em Up, Beat 'Em Down: Kids in Jail

We shot their house up. We shot out their windows. We shot through the door. It was no big deal. It's what I'm used to.

BIG DADDY, 16

I don't care if nobody cares for myself, 'cause I know if somebody cared for me, I wouldn't be in here. See what I'm saying?

TOM CAT, 17

Dewayne, sixteen: "Get a girlfriend, have a house or a car or somethin', have a little money in the bank. Get a job. That's what I expect out of life. Not much."

Dewayne hung himself in a juvenile correctional institution the night before his seventeenth birthday.

Shopping List

---

1 Dead old lady
1 Blood
1 Hunger
1 Famine
1 War
1 Death
1 Rape
1 Pity
1 Bullet
    (slit your veins)
1 Knife
1 Love
1 Bleeding cootie
1 Incest
1 Poverty
    (starvation)
1 Suicide note
1 Hangman's noose
    (and don't forget the bacon)

SEYI PETER-THOMAS, 15

We learned that kids who are in Boys School are just like us. They go to school, they have to do homework, and they have to be in the house by a certain time. It's really no different there except that they have security guards for parents.

Some of the boys told us that some of the reasons that kids get into trouble is because they don't have anything else to do. So they go and commit crimes and wind up in Boys School. They didn't have anything else to do that day—like work or help a neighbor or go see a friend—so they went out and committed a crime.

We interviewed these kids in a cold, damp room at Indiana Boys School. Jimmy, or Big Daddy as he was known there, turned our initial fear of being there to sadness as he spoke. Clad in a blue uniform, he quickly made us forget why he was in there. He showed knowledge and strong emotions in his words. It was hard for us to believe that he had done something so bad as to get him confined. He knew he had made mistakes in his life, but he could not admit that he regretted them.

He wanted a voice. He wanted to talk and to express his feelings and ideas—something that was virtually impossible in confinement. He urged us to come back. He had more to say, he said, more to share. It really wasn't attention he seemed to chase after, it was dignity. He felt he deserved a second chance to be someone.

Chanda Boyden, 15
Randy McDade, 17
Editors

BIG DADDY, 16, INDIANAPOLIS

In my neighborhood, people are getting shot, getting killed, running around. People selling dope every day. They say average life span for a young black male is twenty-one years. Violence is definitely on the rise 'cause ain't nothing getting better. It's probably just always gonna get worse until you teach your kids to do better. Teach your kids.

I'd put more things, like community centers, where the most violence comes from. I'd fix up the basketball courts, you know, give them something to do. I mean, McDonald's ain't kicking it

161

no more on that four-fifty an hour, so you might as well go sell some dope. Where I live, it's a dope ring on every road. You take all them away and give people something to do and it probably would be less violent.

But maybe a world without violence would be stupid 'cause people need something to talk about. I ain't saying it's right to have violence and talk about it, but you never know. Sometimes you need violence to get your point across. I mean, violence was probably meant to be here. He wouldn't have put it here if it weren't. So it's probably here for a reason—wouldn't be writing this book if there was no violence.

We ain't got no relations with the police or nothing like that. Just as long as they go home, they don't care who they hurt or what they do. I mean, look at our little kids growing up, my nieces and nephews, how can they call the officer Mr. Friendly when they got guns all over? If you just go around popping each other, I don't think it'll never change 'cause that's all kids see nowadays. Just that.

Some people make you resort to violence. You gotta prove, you gotta show people violence to show yourself and prove to them that what you mean is business. Like that war Bush started —I mean, that wasn't necessary. Send all them people over there for something that they had nothing to do with. I mean, that didn't make no sense. They said, Support your troops. Forget that, man. I didn't tell them to go over there. That's they fault.

When I got into trouble, I didn't mean to. Just standing around, got into it with this dude. And we was fighting. So I called my cousin up and he came over. He had a sawed-off .14 and so we shot their house up. We shot out their windows and stuff, we shot through the door. I didn't hit nobody, just shot through the house.

It was no big deal. It's what I'm used to. I guess it's my nature, you know, what I grew up to expect to find. I don't expect that much out of life, you know. Like they say, I might not live over twenty-one. Ain't nothin' much to expect. I just try to have fun and enjoy life to the fullest.

I've done lots of violent acts and crimes. Some of them I didn't get caught for. What I was thinking about is scare them, just do something to hurt them. That's all I think about, just hurt them.

I experience violence a lot, a whole lot. It's a lot of violence in my family. A lot of my uncles and stuff are locked up for like five or ten years. My sister's boyfriend is locked up for armed robbery. And me, I'm locked up for possession. Yeah, there's a lot of violence running in my family, probably 'cause of the neighborhood.

I think television is a problem, too. It's too violent, because little kids watch it and they get those images of all those dudes going around shooting up. And then they get out there and do just that. They want to be like the heroes they see in the movies. TV makes it seem so easy. You always get away, but people know that ain't true. Even Tom and Jerry—they go around hitting each other with hammers and stuff. Kids watch that.

When I'm outside I don't go looking for violence, you know. You can survive on the streets without a gun if you can talk good. My mother always told me I have the gift of gab. I can talk my way out of anything. And I ain't ashamed to admit it. I sell dope, but I don't brag on it. People think most dope dudes carry guns. But if they carry a gun when the police come, it's harder to throw a gun than it is to throw something all bagged up. So most of them don't carry a gun. You can talk your way out of anything. You can survive without a gun on the street.

You can kill somebody just as dead with your bare hands. Some people think that if you shoot somebody, that means you a wimp or something, but do it matter after that? I mean he dead, right? So it really don't matter. Maybe guns are for punks, I don't know. He shoot you, you're gone. That's all that really counts. In my neighborhood, violence is real common. Something happens every day.

I think life is what you can make out of it. Anybody can make it better. I ain't forced to sell. I ain't gotta do what I do. I can go to school every day if I wanted to, be a straight-A student 'cause I ain't no dumb person. But it's what you want out of it, what you make out of it. That's how I look at it.

I think things could be a lot worse, a lot more violent. I mean, this ain't nothing of what it could be like. Anything could happen. We could just start playing cowboys with Indians. Everything would be messed up then. Run around shooting people everywhere. That death rate's gonna go up through the roof. To me, don't nobody need to die. I mean, you should give everybody a chance to live. Some people do the wrong things and happen to be at the wrong place at the right time.

Drugs plays a major role, a big part in our problems today. What I see, anybody trying to sell dope, they'll do anything. The bag comes up from Florida, looks like cocaine, *boom,* give it to somebody, give it to little kids, they don't care. Then someone gets upset, they come back, and you start shooting. *Boom.* Somebody shoot your little brother and you go shoot somebody. That's the way it is. Drugs got you all goofed up.

So I don't mess with that stuff. I don't give little kids nothing. The youngest person I ever sold dope to was about eighteen or nineteen. I ain't never sold to nobody my age or any younger. The average person I know who sell dope don't sell dope to kids. But the few people that I buy dope from, you know, they sell dope to me. But I ain't using it. No way, man.

The reason why I do the things that I do is because we ain't never had it good. I do the things I do so I can get paid, so I can look out for myself and help my mother out a lot. We ain't all bad. In a perfect world, there would be good things—more black leaders and everybody just chilling.

I've been asked to join gangs a lot. Said no. I wasn't with it. I mean ain't no purpose in it. Some of them think they was formed to help people out, have something to get into to keep you out of trouble. But then it just got on the wrong track, you know, the wrong way. People don't realize, you know, people are gang-banging here, they want to know how you can benefit they nation? That's the concept for the nation. How would you benefit they nation. Then they go kill this one or that one. No, I can't be with it. It wouldn't be worth it. It's not that great.

If I saw a gang walking down the street, I wouldn't do nothing. I'd keep going about my business. People think 'cause you're in a gang you're always out to hurt and rob people. Ain't all about that, man. I don't gang-bang myself. I don't like gangs. But you know, they ain't all negative. They don't all just go around seeing what they can hurt, hurting people all day long.

Just 'cause you see somebody walking down the street, you gonna run? *No.* That's what the white society put down on our community, they look at us that way like we're gonna do something to them. That's what automatically pops into their head. Well, let me tell you something. We ain't often doing nothing to you. The reason why they do something to you? They see you run and they gonna think, Damn, he wants us to do something to him. That's what happen when they see a black person and they go the other way. That's why things happen to them like that.

If I could change anything about my life, I wouldn't be locked up. I'd change my environment. What I'd like is to live good. Having everything you want, that be living.

But if you think about it, this is a summer camp. This ain't nothing. This is supposed to be Department of Corrections, you know, you come in here and they supposed to show you some kind of way to correct yourself.

I been here twice. I did a year last time. I'm doing about six months this time. This ain't nothing. It's a day camp. When I get out there I probably be back again. It just don't show me no reason to change for except being locked up. But being locked up in here, what do I gotta worry about? I mean nothing. Seem like we safe. This is what my mother said in court, you know. She said at least if I'm being in here she know where I'm at. This probably help my mother sleep at night knowing that I'm safe somewhere.

Here in this place, with the lieutenants and stuff, the chief supervisor, they mess with us, so we gotta watch our back with them every day. They keep sweating us all the time and when we come to school, we got people always peeping and watching you out. You go to class, say as less as possible to those people so they can't mess with you.

I fight to solve mostly all my problems, either argumentative or physically. I love it. It's exciting. If I see somebody fighting, I be saying, Get him, kick him, beat him up. If somebody fighting that I don't like and I think I can get away with it, I kick him myself. It don't really bother me, it don't make me sad or nothing. I get a kick out of it.

I just really want to be rich. I'll get it any way I can for real, but I won't steal, though. I wouldn't steal nothing from nobody. Sometimes I go in a store and I'm ready to steal a piece of candy and I get scared for real. If I can go out, I go out and sell dope, but steal a piece of candy make me scared and nervous and I be shaking. I'd put it in my pocket and get up there and pay for it. It gets to me. I don't know.

One time, when I was thirteen, I was doing real good and I counted five thousand dollars and it was mine. Something that I made and didn't nobody give it to me. That felt good to know that you got out there and got it yourself. When you got money, right, I mean you got money. A dollar ain't nothing. You give a dollar out to your little niece, like nothing, *boom*.

But then when you broke, the first thing you want is a dollar. I mean, let me get a dollar, man, let me work with a dollar. And that's bad, boy. I like doing things, you know, never having to ask nobody for nothing. My fear is of dying and being broke, having no money at all for real.

It's bad being locked up and away from your family. 'Cause you want to do good things and do stuff positive. You want to be good all your life, hopefully. I describe myself as a very intelligent individual, a very street-wise young individual. Some people are really scared of me for real, but I ain't a bad person. I mean, you wouldn't know me unless you've seen me personally.

Just 'cause we in here don't mean we all bad. Some of it come from what we live in and what we used to, what we adapted to, you know. Some of it is our way of life. People look at me like, He's a menace to society. They say we don't do nothing to society but pollute it. But maybe that's all I know and nobody tried to teach me better. My mother, even, my mother's the only person I ever had to really look out for me.

I think my kids gonna have it great 'cause they can see how I messed up and what I've been through. They can learn. And I'm gonna teach them what it's like on the streets. I'm just gonna teach them all the good things and what to stay away from and teach them ideas. I'll encourage them to go out there and do nothing wrong. I ain't gonna let them sit here and be in La-La Land, you know, thinking everything out there is hurt, 'cause it ain't. But it's rough, you know. I hope by the time I have kids I'll be out of the ghetto. That's where I stay at, the ghetto.

And so that's really why I do the things that I do. People say I could change if I want to, if I know a lot of stuff. I know I can get in anything if I really wanted to, but they don't never give me reason to change for. That's probably why I do the things I do.

We interviewed Tom Cat in a six-by-six-foot room that seemed more like a jail cell than a visiting room at the Juvenile Detention Center in Indianapolis. The detention center is very modern and very secure.

Tom Cat had loosely curled, short hair and his right arm was in a sling. Ringlets framed his handsome, youthful face. He wore a T-shirt and pants. His eyes were sweet but mischievous, and they darted around the room and through the glass to the room outside.

Several times during the interview Tom Cat was told by his supervisor, who stood at the other side of the cell's glass window, to stop tipping his chair back. Every time the supervisor turned his back, Tom Cat would give him the finger and tip his chair back.

Tom Cat was a smart, charismatic, articulate, likable, funny person. He was a leader and the role model to two others who we interviewed with him. But he also was self-destructive and impulsive. I think he probably was very self-centered, too.

Kathleen Hustad, 17, Editor

TOM CAT, 17, INDIANAPOLIS

TOM: I'm in here for murder.

CE: Uh-uh. No you're not. First, tell me your name, what do you want to be called?

TOM: Mike Tyson. Nah, it's really Tom. Tom Cat.

CE: And what are you in here for, Tom?

TOM: Possession and two disorderly conducts, assault and battery on a police officer. I've been at Boys School four times.

CE: Why did you do that?

TOM: Well, I don't like the police and I got a bad sympathy on authority. I don't like authority figures at all, besides my mom. And the police, you know, they think they can get away with

168

scot-free murder. I've seen people get beat up, shot at, dope taken from police, police don't lock them up. I've seen it all. But when it comes down to them messing with me, I feel that if they can play with fire, I can play with fire back. So I get my thrills off of me being who I want to be and I don't take no B.S. from nobody.

I feel if a person does something that he did at the time, you know, he paid his price and did his time. I don't feel that he should be bothered with no more. But the police get it to where once you did something wrong, you gonna always do something wrong. No ifs and buts, no questions asked.

And that's the kind of reputation I got to where I done did so much in my past that if my name pop up on a screen across one of these police things, then automatically they gonna say I did it. Even if I'm in my neighborhood and something happens, they gonna come to me 'cause I'm the one that got the record. They gonna automatically accuse me of doing it until they find somebody else to take over my reputation.

CE: Do you think your rights are being taken advantage of because you're a minor?

TOM: Not actually, because I'll be eighteen next Wednesday and at my age I will be going to Marion County Jail. I never accuse myself of being a minor even from my younger age. Because I ain't had a father when I grew up. I had a stepfather but not a real father that's gonna love me and comfort me and really sit down and do for me. I ain't never had that type of person. All I had was a mother, so I felt I was man of myself. That's why I've been getting locked up when I was young because I didn't accept no authority because I never had a father figure.

CE: So how many cars do you think you've stolen?

TOM: In my whole life? I can't even name it. I used to steal about five cars in one day.

CE: Does ripping off cars make more money than dope?

TOM: No, we do that, too.

CE: It's like once you get all that money in your pocket you don't want to quit?

TOM: You get that feeling. I once had so much money, it was in boxes up to my knees. I seen about eight boxes coming out of one room filled with just money. It's the most money I ever seen.

CE: How do you get that kind of money?

TOM: Selling dope. Big quantities. Not just little piece by piece, eight bottles, sixteens, quarters, or shit like that. I'm talking quantities. You know, like forty-five thousand dollars' worth of 'caine in a day. You see what I'm saying?

CE: So how do you transport the dope? In gangs? Are you part of gangs? You want to talk about that?

TOM: Yeah. I want to talk about gangs. I been in a gang almost all my life.

CE: Are you a Disciple?

TOM: I'm Straight Up Folks.

CE: I've heard about that. You're supposed to be a family, right? Is that the one?

TOM: Yeah. See, most gangs talk—they say Vice Lords, they disrespected as gumbo bellies, vicki lous, mary lou tops, all of that. But we more organization, you know, one big family. We all believe in two things and two things only: making money

170

and sticking up for one another. That's what we consider ourselves. If we see a Vice Lord and he disrespect one of us, he might as well disrespect *every* one of us 'cause we all is more of one family.

My branch is totally different from other people's. Some people, they gladiate, you know, for disrespect. Some people will shoot a person in his chest, shoot him in the head. That's they branch. If you disrespected, you must violate.

I live on the West Side, I lived there damn near all my life. I done seen damn near almost every gun there is that's been around. You know, from a .30-30 to a .30-06, from a nine-millimeter to a naked special. A naked special is three-piece set on a .38.

I seen little kids running around with no shoes on, their parents can't afford to buy them shoes in the project. I seen all that. And you know, it's not just because that's how they grew up. It's because of their parents, growing up with the lifestyle. If they can get a job that's gonna pay them, then their kids wouldn't grow up being like that. But if you're only making a hundred and twenty-five dollars a week, where can you stay at? I mean, the only place you can stay at is a low-rent welfare, all your life, letting government help you out. And they just don't understand.

It's not— I mean, I'm gonna be honest. I'm not prejudice. My mom's white, my father's Puerto Rican and black. So we're all separated. We supposed to be equal, but it don't seem like it.

You come in our neighborhood talking shit, you either got two positions. You either leave in a box or you leave and go to the hospital. You make your own decision. If you bring trouble on yourself, you should be able to take the additional ass kickings. These guys came over from the East Side, came to our side thinking they can tear it up. They Vice Lords. They think they can come to our side and do what they want to do. They wrong about that. I shot one of them in the back.

CE: Why did you shoot the guy in the back?

171

TOM: Wasn't nothing else to do. I shot a lot of people. Once I shot somebody three times. I was drunk. I was drunk straight out and I was smoking weed, too. This dude spit on my car, so I got out, pulled my pistol, and asked him why he did it. And I put the pearl in his mouth. He got scared, so I just pulled it out and said, Fuck you—*pop, pop, pop*. Don't know where I shot, I just shot. *Pop, pop*, that's all you heard. And he shot me in the ass.

CE: So why did you join a gang?

TOM: I got it from two of my cousins, I experienced it from them, they stole cars. They in the penitentiary now. When I was eight years old, I knew how to steal a car. Now that's bad. I just didn't know how to drive. I used to steal cars for the heck of it and teach myself, I taught myself how to drive. And ever since, I get my thrills off of doing my cousin's nation. I get it in my head to where I want to be that. I get my thrills off of doing it to them. If they can do it to me, I can do it back to them. I get my thrills off of building my brain. Sitting down with one of my folks, talking about the good times and what we gonna do on Judgment Day.

I don't care if nobody cares for myself, 'cause I know if somebody cared for me, I wouldn't be here. See what I'm saying? I know the law don't care for me, 'cause if they did, I wouldn't be here. So why should I care for the law? That's how I feel.

I always said if I ever get locked up, I'm gonna get locked up for murder. It was in my mind. And if I kill one person, I know I'm gonna get life. So I might as well, every person I see I don't like, just *pop*, shoot my old pistol, *pop, pop*. That's why if I had a murder charge, might as well get about ninety of them. I know it's gonna take them all this time to get me 'cause they ain't gonna catch me.

CE: Why don't they catch you?

TOM: They take the longest. But I know I'm gonna be doing life, so I might as well get more out while I can. Get all the sex

172

in the world, drink all the liquor I can get, smoke all the weed I can smoke, just do what I can do. And before they catch me, I probably will kill my own self before I let them catch me. 'Cause I know I'm gonna do life. I'm gonna die in prison, so I might as well go on ahead and before I let them do me, I might as well kill my own self. I'm tired of being locked up.

CE: I'm sure nobody likes being locked up. Why do you go back?

TOM: Ain't nothin' to do. Ain't nothin' to turn to. You go to boys' clubs, you get in a fight because of your reputation. If you try to get a job, somebody gonna come get a job messing with you and they ain't gonna like it. So you mess around, get a battery, and you don't got a job. Most people in my neighborhood don't want to work in no fast-food restaurant, anyway. So somebody want to make it big, they gonna make it big the best way they can. That's either slaying, or gang-banging, or taking somebody money.

But, like they say, you still a baby and you locked up as a baby. You ain't gonna have nothing to live for. You seventeen years old and you gonna do thirty, forty years, and you get out when you sixty? Look at all you missed. Look at all you missed. I mean, you still need a childhood. You ain't been in love yet. You haven't felt love. You haven't made no babies. You ain't had no job and experienced life hardly at all. What you gonna do? You gonna go to the penitentiary, you gonna be like, This is my home now.

All you gonna be doing is be a fag, you know. You ain't be able to enjoy life. Only life you gonna enjoy is him giving me a piece of his sex life and me taking his dinner tray. That's all I can look up for. Wake up every morning and say, I'm living, I ain't been sinked yet. I might as well go on ahead and take what belongs to me. He's in my part of the cell and this is my cell. If he come in my cell, he gotta at least pay me rent. If I had my own cell and I been there five or ten years already and I knew I got some more years until I be seventy, and if a man came to

173

my cell, I'd say straight out, Hey, you can call me a fag, but hey, my hormones is at least gonna get pleased. I mean, I'll be honest.

CE: How do you think we can make the world less violent?

TOM: Take all the blacks out.

CE: No, come on.

TOM: I mean it, take all the blacks out. 'Cause if you got one rotten apple in the bunch, it's gonna spoil the whole bunch. So if you got one black ass, you know one black person that's gonna act his color, then . . .

CE: Aren't some white people violent, too?

TOM: Well, most white people I've seen, they like to get high, get drunk, maybe to have fun. A lot of them just like to act like assholes, but if you see violence on TV, ninety percent it's a black person starting it.

CE: But that's on TV, that's not real life.

TOM: I've been to a lot of parties in my life. I've been to white parties and all I seen was them getting drunk, getting high, chicks having sex with a guy in a car and stuff like that.
   I've been to the black-person party and all I seen was shootouts, fights, and everybody smoking weed and hitting the pipe or something like that. So tell me the difference. Which party would you like to go to? Thank you.

Over the summer of 1992, we had a chance to meet an eighteen-year-old girl named Leigh. She has a loving family, just like us. She likes music and writing, just like us. She has hopes and dreams, just like us. The difference is we are here writing this, and she is sitting in an Oklahoma jail convicted of two counts of murder and sentences to two consecutive life terms.

She is not a child of the problems of today's society. She didn't grow up in a bad neighborhood. Her parents didn't beat her and she wasn't raped. She is a young eighteen-year-old who couldn't get along with her parents.

Before we actually saw Leigh, we envisioned a mean and hard-looking female, dressed in a bright orange prison uniform. We first saw her when she was brought in for her preliminary hearing in a small Oklahoma courthouse. She has long blond hair, pale skin, and was dressed in a plaid shirt and pants. Even though she didn't look like we thought she would, we were still scared and intimidated.

Once we started to talk to her, however, our fear slipped away. It became hard to imagine that this girl had committed two cold-blooded murders.

The most amazing thing that happened to us while on this interview was sitting on one side of the bars while Leigh sat on the floor opposite us, telling us that the floor was actually more comfortable than her bed. We began to actually relate to her and her words. We were very closed-minded going into that interview because of stereotypes we had been exposed to, but when we finished we actually began to understand her and sympathize with her. It is something we will never forget.

We finally, for the first time in our lives, learned that unacceptance is part of our violence problem.

Michelle Evans, 17
Erin Cox, 15
Editors

LEIGH ANN, 18, MIAMI, OKLAHOMA

If you don't know what started your problems in the first place, you can't get help. My parents always put a lot of pressure on me. I have a younger sister that gets better grades than I do. I could have got really good grades if I would have just put forth the effort.

I became rebellious as a way of getting attention, I guess. I want to be my own person. I'm real independent and I have my own views and my own opinions and I think my own way. My family didn't want me to do that. I ran away from home when I was fifteen. That was the first time I wound up in Indiana Girls School.

I probably had one of the worst self-images of anybody in there. I hated myself. And you know, I really couldn't even tell you why I did. Me and my parents used to not get along at all. And it's not that we really didn't love each other, we just didn't communicate. We fought. My parents were the same way and so I used to hide all my feelings. I wouldn't talk about them to anybody. So it caused a lot of friction between us when it came to talking stuff out. At the time, I didn't feel like I had anybody that cared.

When I was in Girls School, at least the first two times, we still didn't communicate. We got along okay while I was in there, but then as soon as I'd get released and then go back living under the same roof, we would never get along. We just didn't talk about stuff. About the biggest conversation we had was, Hi, how was your day? Fine. I mean, that was it. Or maybe, What's for dinner? That type of stuff. Nobody talked about anything.

I hardly had any friends in public school, so it was hard to go back. You feel kind of left out because you don't want to go back to the friends that you had before, but the people you want to be friends with and you think would be good for you won't have anything to do with you. I was kind of a loner.

Then I got pregnant. My parents wanted me to get an abortion but I didn't want to. After I found out I was pregnant, I stopped running wild. That forced me to grow up a lot. I mean, from before I got pregnant, I'm a completely different person. I had the baby in an unwed mothers' home and gave up custody of it nine days later. After I had my baby is when my parents

176

and me started communicating, because I started making an effort and they started making an effort.

I learned a lot in Girls School, but I didn't use everything I learned there. If I used everything, I probably wouldn't be here. But I'm not bitter. I let myself get in trouble and I'll pay the price. I just think that people should do all they can to improve their own self-esteem and have respect for oneself. Feeling bad about oneself is, or can be, the root to many problems.

I just wish that everyone that's getting in trouble now could know all that I go through and have gone through, to know how it really feels not to know if someone may sign a death warrant for you in the near future. To not know the next time you'll be able to feel sunlight and walk freely, and to be incarcerated indefinitely. To be a thousand miles away from all you care about and hold dear. All I can do now is listen to music, read, and write poetry. Here is part of a poem I wrote the other day:

> *Lying hopeless tears are falling,*
> *Feeling helpless, what to do?*
> *Keep on working to find the answers,*
> *Turning failure to dreams come true.*
> *The curtain closes, is the act finished?*
> *Am I not doomed as sorrow's bride?*
> *My role has meaning, and life continues,*
> *A happy ending, to know you've tried.*

We interviewed Andrew and Bud at the Sasha Bruce House for runaways in Northeast Washington, D.C. The house sits on a hill in a decrepit neighborhood. The interview took place in a counseling room with a one-way mirror.

Before the interview, we were told that Andrew and Bud had been charged with a crime and wouldn't be allowed to answer any questions about their crime. Needless to say, we were quite nervous when they walked into the room.

They spoke in low, husky voices, but were extremely forthcoming about their experiences. Our mouths hung open with shock as they described the violent acts they had had to endure. We tried to relate to their situation, but none of us had ever had something as terrible as being jailed happen to us. We could only speak about getting pulled over for speeding, while they spoke about getting taken to jail, witnessing murders, and being robbed.

It was really amazing what those kids had been through. One of them had a kid and he was only sixteen, and they were busted for cocaine when they were only twelve. They didn't really have a home. They saw their friends getting shot, everyone having guns. They had some fresh ideas about how to stop the violence that has taken over their neighborhoods.

In a place where it is every man for himself, Andrew and Bud said they were more concerned with where they will be tomorrow than where they will be ten years from now. One of the most disheartening things was that they seemed to be adjusted to all the violence around them; they weren't horrified by the killings or the robberies that occurred. To them, these were just things that happened.

Adam Reichman, 17
Brian Kelley, 17
Anji Rady, 17
Michelle Evans, 18
Editors

ANDREW, 17, AND BUD, 15, WASHINGTON, D.C.

CE: Tell us about yourselves.

ANDREW: My name is Andrew and I'm seventeen. You want to know about violence in D.C.?

CE: Yeah, your experience.

ANDREW: They're not faking out there. It is wild. People are getting killed now, every day. They ain't faking no more.

BUD: My name is Bud, I'm fifteen. I'd say the violence is basically over money, drugs, and girls.

ANDREW: It's more over girls.

CE: They're killing each other over girls?

ANDREW: Yeah, they killing over anything nowadays—to become a man.

CE: Are there a lot of gangs here?

BUD: No, they don't have that gang thing no more.

ANDREW: It's everybody for their self now.

CE: How does it make you feel, witnessing all these people getting shot? How do you feel about that?

ANDREW: I feel lousy, ever since one of my friends got shot over drugs. We was just talking with friends, walking up and down the street. We don't have nothing to do, you know.

BUD: One day I went out and got into trouble during lunch hour. It was a mess. They almost locked me out. This guy was working at McDonald's. It wasn't like a violent thing, but it was just— Well, he hit me. He kept on running off at the mouth. And then he came out with a ladder and he hit one of my friends across the back with the ladder. So they got in a fight. I stepped back and was just standing there watching, and then the police came and they grabbed everybody.

CE: Do the police mess with you?

ANDREW: That's the big thing whenever you see the police. I mean, it's like five or six of us, we're all just standing there, pointing at something. They would actually stop and first try to run you in. Then they'll tell you to leave, for no reason. Then they'll drive up the street and catch one of y'all when you be by yourself, write your name down, cuss you out, and treat you like dirt.

Just because they got a badge and a gun. They don't think they're the same anymore. They get this rank, they forget where they come from. You say something to them and they put you in handcuffs. They tell you, you talk anything smart, they gonna bust you in your mouth. They threaten and they don't care what you say.

They kill people. They killing little kids. But they not doing nothing for the people.

CE: What would you say to the President if you could talk to him about it?

ANDREW: I would tell him, Man, take the D.C. police off the street. It's much better if you do that. They could put the National Guard out in this joint, man.

Whatever happened to the Guardian Angels? They got tired, they don't want them marshalls out there. Marshalls beat you up. They gonna beat you up on the corner, man.

CE: Do you think violence is on the rise? Do you think you'll get more of it?

ANDREW: Yeah, you get more of it now than ever. But it's mostly young ones—young people are doing all the violent crime. There's a whole bunch of it, over petty stuff—they just don't like the way you looked at them, stuff like that.

CE: What would you do to make the world less violent?

ANDREW: If I had the power, if I was the President and I had the power, I'd bring the electric chair back for the ones that's killing people.

BUD: We have it here in D.C., but they ain't using it. They ain't using it at all. I'd have an army walking on the streets instead of the police. I'd have an army out there. Public hangings.

ANDREW: That's it. Everybody come down to the public monument, watch somebody get thrown off the top of the monument. You want to kill somebody, some guy selling drugs, I'd do that to him.

I'd send them down across the sea to fight the war. If they want to use a gun so bad, send them right across the seas. Put them on the first boat to Nicaragua or somewhere. Won't have to worry about them fighting no more when they come back. They won't even want to hold a gun no more.

CE: Is there anywhere safe to go without a gun?

BUD: Virginia.

ANDREW: Not even Virginia. Nowhere's safe anymore. Like around here, you can't even walk on a public avenue without somebody trying to get bucks.

BUD: You got like five or ten people up in one small little car, just ready to start something with somebody.

CE: How are the girls as far as violence is concerned?

ANDREW: They're the cause of violence. I mean, they fight, too. Or sometimes if you're overprotective, you don't want anybody looking at your girl, you might look at somebody the wrong way and they might come up and say something smart and *boom,* they leave you dead.

CE: Has violence become ordinary to you, accepted by you?

ANDREW: To me, for real, it has become ordinary. When you turn on the TV, you hear the news, you hear about somebody that got gunned down in their car, or you got somebody shooting down people.

It's beginning to get a lot. Every morning, if you get a D.C. paper for a week, you'll see every day, two or three kids, somebody got killed in the last twenty-four hours, overnight.

You go down in Southeast, man, they would try everything in their power. They'll walk past you and scope you out first. Then they'll bump you and grab you or hit you. Then this whole gang of them just come in.

BUD: They shoot.

ANDREW: They stick a gun in your mouth, right then, and tell you to give it up. You ain't got nothing, you put your feet up and hope they let you go.

BUD: That's the best you can hope. If you ain't got no money, sometimes they might let you go. I mean, even if you do have money, sometimes they won't let you go.

ANDREW: And plus, they'll hit you in the head with a gun, they gonna knock you out. You gonna come back and get them?

BUD: Some people say it's gonna stop. But I don't think it's gonna stop. I think it's gonna get worser and worser.

CE: Have you ever had a time in your life when there wasn't any violence?

ANDREW: Yeah, when I was a baby. Then I ain't knowing nothing about violence.

CE: Have you ever had a crime committed against you?

ANDREW: Yeah, I got stuck up plenty of times, by people I don't even know. I'm just walking down the street. They run up behind me and put a gun in my chin and pull me to the side. That's why I don't carry no money on me anymore. You're scared when you get robbed, man. You're scared.

CE: What happens in school? Is school safe?

ANDREW: It's as safe as it is in the street. In school you get all the hustlers, they go to school. They go to school to look good and to try to impress the girls. They bring guns to school, drugs, they bring basically everything to school.

BUD: Anywhere you go, there's gonna be crime. You go to the mall, walk through the mall, you see one girl standing by herself. You go up to her to talk to her and *boom,* you see her boyfriend coming back and five other guys, ready to jump you for just saying hello to the girl. If they think you got money, they try robbing.

CE: What would you say to somebody who's about to shoot somebody? What would you say to make them not shoot that person?

BUD: There's nothing that you really could say if somebody's trying to shoot someone. Because it's in their head that they want them dead.

ANDREW: But then again, you might get a person that will listen to you. Or they might go back out that night when you're not around. You really can't stop a depressed person.

CE: What was the first crime you committed?

ANDREW: My first was a little misdemeanor charge. I think it was acting up on the streets or something like that. It's not like I commit a crime every day, you know.

CE: How old were you?

ANDREW: Sixteen. It was a while before I pulled my first job.

CE: What was that?

ANDREW: Unauthorized use of a vehicle.

BUD: Stolen car.

CE: What was yours?

BUD: Coke.

CE: How old were you?

BUD: Fourteen.

CE: What was it like, getting locked up?

ANDREW: When I first got locked up, it was seriously a joke to me, really. I'm not gonna lie. It was a joke to me. But the second time I got locked up and they sent me away for a couple of months, it wasn't no joke anymore. I was ready to go home then.

CE: What was it like in there?

ANDREW: When I first got out there, I didn't know a soul. It's like you're lost. There ain't nobody to say nothing to, so I stayed by myself. Then I got to coming down here, back and forth, every six months or so, and I got to know everybody down there. Then it was more fun.

But then you get to thinking, You could be out there with your girlfriend, out there really having fun, and it's not gonna be fun inside no more.

BUD: It was all right, but next time I started thinking about my kid. Before I get home, it seem like they send me back down.

CE: Some people say when you go to jail it just teaches you how to be a better criminal, it doesn't rehabilitate you.

ANDREW: It makes you think about what you did. You don't do it the same way no more.

BUD: But some of them, it do make you think about being a better criminal. Some of them boys are down there with a big head. They did big crimes, like running up against stores, stealing a car, robbing Safeway, stuff like that. They tell you how to do it.

CE: Where do you see yourself ten years from now?

BUD: I ain't never thought about it, really.

CE: What's more important, ten years from now or tomorrow?

BUD: Tomorrow.

ANDREW: Who cares about ten years from now? You living day by day.

BUD: You can't look too far ahead. Go too far ahead, you gone. You look ahead ten years, next day, somebody takes you out.

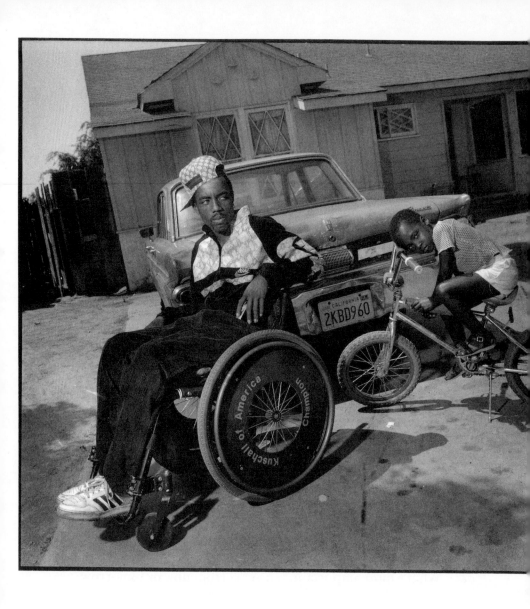

"Six Pack Rapper," nineteen, was paralyzed by gang violence in L.A.

7

Los Angeles: Unanswered Tears

If it wasn't for that man with the video camera, could you imagine the trial? They'd probably be like, Oh, come on now. How did you really get these bruises?

JAZZ, 16

Out of all the funerals, I never seen a father right there, crying. Only the moms, crying and crying and crying at the funerals and afterwards.

MARIA, 16

At my church there was a lot of blacks coming in or we'd go to black churches and try to break the barrier. This is the first time we're really actually trying to understand one another.

KIM, 17

Death

Lightning flashes
Flesh is torn
People scream red rain falls

Sirens flare
tears fall making puddles
on the ground

The rain comes
on that dreary day
people put their memories away

Ryan Fischer, 14

When we were in L.A. we went to this place called The Allen House. It was across the street from the AME church, and that's where we met these gang members. That's where they go and do work for the community. They clean the streets. It's like a youth corps. I think they also talk about the problems that they have.

So that's where I got to meet Jazz. He was black, but he wasn't too dark. He had like hazel eyes and long, curly hair. It wasn't nothing like Jeri curls, but somewhat like tiny dreds. He was slim and pretty tall. I really liked him.

He had an attitude about how the gangs were rough and stuff and I knew he was involved already. But he knew right from wrong. He had values. He got them from his mom, I think, he wants to look out for her. So he's trying to calm down.

I was extremely nervous when I first went over 'cause it was me alone with eight guys and I thought they might try and kill me. But then I got all their names and started talking to them about what they did and I felt more comfortable. I made friends with them. If I lived in L.A., I would go over to that group and see them once in a while. They were really cool people.

Hector Cruzado, 15, Editor

JAZZ, 16

What I do most of the time is tap and strut—dancing—and write on walls. Get different styles. I've been dancing since I was born because that's what I like. I dance into my house, I include it in my life, I take it to a club, and damn, I look pretty smooth.

My childhood, I guess, wasn't all that good because once I got like eleven years old people started trying to persuade me to go other ways—like, Let's do this and you should join that and be down with this.

I didn't want to do no gang because a lot of fools would get shot over dumb shit—like over the color of your shoelaces. Some fool wears some red shoelaces and they go down the street and *bam*, they gone. But now it's calmed down some, people are starting to realize, Damn, man, that shit was dumb, you know, we should calm this down because I'm tired of my brother getting killed, my father getting killed, my uncle getting killed. You know that's not even right.

Just this month, my homeboy had a stolen car, a G ride—you know, GTA, grand thief auto. Police had chased him on this G ride and when he stopped and pulled across a lawn and started to run, the police shot him in the back seven times. And they handcuffed him and they hog-tied him, tied his legs with his knee all the way back, and he's already shot and bleeding to death. Even when the ambulance come, they still didn't want to untie him. He's shot seven times in the back, man, he ain't goin' nowhere. No need to hog-tie him.

But that's like an everyday thing in L.A., it's always some Hispanic, some black, never a Caucasian getting killed. It's always the minorities getting fucked over. You know you can't walk into a store without somebody following you behind your back looking like he worried you gonna steal something. I got money in my pocket to buy whatever I want. That makes me feel like, Damn, man, like I got a name on me there that I didn't even put there and that ain't right. When I walk into places, ladies hold their purses close to them because I'm a black male. I'm thinking, Lady, I don't want your purse because, you know, that's not me. It's stupid, man. It's like a fucked-up stereotype. That's all it is.

I was put away last year. Three months because me and my homies went out and we got drunk or whatever and we were kicking in towards Beverly Hills and I was fading, I was gone. But then this white male, this hustler, started to bullshit us. He had this dog and he came after us, shouting, You goddamn niggers get out of my neighborhood. So I just beat his ass and he pressed charges against me. That wasn't even right. I mean, his dog could have bit us and we could have as easily pressed charges against him. But then the charges were dropped and I had three months in the California Youth Center. But it was really only two months because then I got put on probation. I had to report to this probation officer, it's like your freedom is taken away from you.

What about the L.A. riots? I felt like people had a lot of things on their chest—and they still do got a lot of things on their chest—and the riots just brought a lot of that stuff out. It wasn't just a black thing. It was a respect thing. You saw Puerto Ricans, Hispanics, all kinds of minorities together. It wasn't one race doing one thing. It was all races doing everything. People were joined together. It was a unity thing.

You know, Rodney King had his faults, like before, or whatever, and he didn't stop the car. But just because of that they didn't have to beat him the way they did. Say if it was the reverse situation, if it was fifteen black cops beating up on one white guy. You better believe they'd be behind bars right now doing some years.

I didn't even feel it was so bad to have the trial be in Simi Valley because if they had had it down here, it would have been worse. But I thought at least the jury was going to be mixed up instead of all white.

If it wasn't for that man with the video camera, could you imagine the trial? They'd probably be like, Oh, come on now. How did you really get these bruises? Did you beat yourself and try to blame it on the police officers or did you just happen to have a car accident before? Or something like this. They'd have probably joked it all around and made the black man feel foolish.

The law's supposed to be the law, but they breaking the law theyselves. It could have been prevented if they were sentenced and got whatever they had coming to them, like a fair trial. Then the riot would have never happened, nobody would have got beat, no places would have been burnt, and L.A. would need no money to rebuild nothing because nothing would have been destroyed. You know the lawmakers saw this coming and they did nothing about it. They knew it was going to happen and they let it happen.

But I don't think they should be brought back to trial now because what's done is done. We shouldn't go back to the problem, we should just build from what we have now.

I see great things for my future because I came out of junior high school with honors. Even though I dance a lot, in the wintertime my dancing is cut down to a limit because my books come first. In my family there's always a study period that you got to go to. My school now is in Santa Monica, three blocks from UCLA. I'm studying mathematics.

And you know, that's another thing that's wrong. They don't give you the chance to show your intelligence 'cause they got the stereotype on you. But I think if you would take some of these white boys off the streets and not have an IQ test but give them a test on different stuff based on life, I think you know that that person up the street will have enough smarts to come out on top because a white boy, he just knows what people teach him. That's the problem with white people, they only know what you teach them. But I tend to expand my horizons by going further than they teach me. For instance, in high school now we have no black history. Our black history comes like once a month, sometimes at the end of January or towards February. February's Black History Month and it's the shortest month. They give us the shortest month out of the whole year.

We met Maria in Compton. It was a very hot day and I was kind of scared because we'd heard a lot of bad stuff about Compton, like if you step into someone's territory, you're gone.

We met Maria on the street. She was a young girl, she's Mexican. She was real pretty. She talked about what all the different groups do, what the black people do, what the Hispanics do. She told me a lot about their parties, what she be doing when she hangs out. She was very open.

I liked her accent. It was real nice, different from the girls in New York. The girls in New York are kind of rough, but Maria was very sweet.

Eric Zamora, 16, Editor
with Rolando Liriano, 16, Editor

MARIA, 16

CE: So tell me, Maria, do you hang out a lot?

MARIA: I go to a lot of parties. Sometimes they're all right, but then when them gangsters start coming, well, the party ends and that's it. You can't party no more because they'll all start shooting.

There's a lot of gang-banging in my neighborhood and the walls are really nasty. It's so stupid 'cause when one writes, then the other ones come and cross it out, and then the other one comes and it's just scribble scrabble all over the wall. And they just kill each other when they see them, they get jumped and then they shoot them. You hear the shots. That's it.

CE: What was it like when you were younger?

MARIA: It was calmer then, but now little kids are already in the gang. When I was little, actually, I used to kick back with the Bloods. When I used to go to the park, they were always there. It was scary 'cause they wear red, and if anyone passes wearing blue, you just see everybody running, hiding, 'cause if they don't hide, they just get shot.

CE: Do you live with your mother and father?

MARIA: I live with my mom and my dad, but he's not really like my dad 'cause he be drinking all the time.

CE: Do you want to move out?

MARIA: Yeah, I ran away from the house so many times. I go to a party, to a movie, to them drive-ins, get drunk, smoke, that's it.

CE: Haven't you ever thought of your family getting worried?

MARIA: No, 'cause they never did. I don't think so. Out of all the times I ran away, they only called the police one time. But they didn't catch me. The police don't even bother looking for you. I came back by my own.

CE: So you think the cops are not responsible?

MARIA: No. 'Cause if they was, they would have catched me.

CE: Who do you think is responsible for all this, I mean the L.A. riots?

MARIA: The police. How was they just gonna beat on Rodney King like that and not do nothing about it? Them cops always be trying to beat up on somebody. All the time. And you don't ever see no whites getting beat up on. You only see blacks and Mexicans right there on the floor. That's all. They're all gangsters, with all them drive-by shootings and the killings and all.

CE: Do you know anyone that got killed?

MARIA: Yeah, all my homeboys. Like five or six of them from the Seminoles. The youngest one was fifteen. They used to go to Robert F. Kennedy and Compton High and after that they just died. They stopped going to school and started gang-banging and they just died. They shot them. Their enemies.

CE: How was it for their families?

MARIA: Well, their moms were just crying and crying and crying, like at the funeral and afterwards. Practically never was the dad there, though, only the moms.

CE: So why not the dads? What were the fathers doing?

MARIA: I don't know. I guess they just tired, they leave, they don't care. Out of all the funerals, I never seen a father right there, crying.

CE: So what is missing in this community?

MARIA: Police, I guess. They need to stop the gangs. If it wasn't for no gangs, there would have been a lot of people here still.
   We need to have more sports, too, more things for the teenagers so they wouldn't be in gangs. That's why they need gangs, 'cause there ain't nothing to do, so you might as well be in the street if there ain't nothing to do. They might as well just go jump somebody or kill somebody. They just do it so that they can think they're hard. So they could have their respect all the time.

CE: What was it like during the riot? It looked like people were just going berserk, all the fires and all the people dying. Were you scared?

MARIA: I wasn't scared 'cause it happens all the time. You always hear people dying or going to jail.

CE: Don't people ever talk or think about their future?

MARIA: No. They don't have a future.

We went to talk to Kim, a Korean girl, and her family in her home. I've never seen such a beautiful neighborhood in my life. The houses were outstanding. When we went into her house, we actually had to take off our shoes. I only saw this on TV, I never knew it was going to happen to me in real life. So I know that was a real strong culture they had there.

Inside the house was very ornate—beautiful furniture, very clean, TV, everything. Kim's mother served us juice and fruits, Korean grapes; they were real good. They all were very hospitable, they made us feel like we were part of the family.

Kim is very beautiful. Beautiful and very smart. She feels real sad and kind of messed up about her father's store burning down in the riots. I felt bad for her because she talked about how before this had happened, they used to take things for granted and now she learned, you know, that it's not good to do that because now she's living on a minimum. She can't have what she used to have before. She was taking her upper-middle-class lifestyle that her family worked so hard for for granted and now they have nothing. She was very sad about the whole deal.

But she wasn't resentful of black people. She was just angry that it happened. She said she has black friends and she feels closer to them now since the riots. She's very Christian. She talked about how at church the priest is black and he apologized for all, on behalf of, his black people.

So the Chang family looks very wealthy, but if the insurance company doesn't pay, they don't know what they're going to do. I wish them the best of luck to cope with their problems about their father's business going down.

Eric Zamora, 16, Editor
with Rolando Liriano, 16, Editor

KIM, 17

I was born in Korea and I came here over twelve years ago. I'm going to be a senior at Downey High. We don't really have crimes or anything in this neighborhood, but I think there's a lot of victims of the riot. Many were hurt by it and some lost a lot of money. They were pretty much very saddened by everything.

Like for our family, my dad's supermarket got all burned down. There's nothing left after the riot. That's the only thing they have, that's all of their money invested and everything. His whole American dream is all burned down the drain now. And the problem is that our insurance company said they don't have enough money and they can't cover what we lost. So now we don't know what to do. We're pretty much angry. And sort of scared, too.

I know a lot of Koreans, a lot of victims of the riots, that might turn against the blacks. They might say, Oh my God, we're so angry at them, how could they do this to us, destroying everything? But my dad is very open-minded. And I agree. I don't think we have to blame it on the blacks.

I think the whole society is to blame, and I'm angry. The whole community, and the majority is white, they totally ignore the issue because it's not involving them. I'm angry at that. There's so many killed, so many families ruined. There's so many things going wrong and they don't even care for it, they don't sympathize with what's happening, with the blacks *or* the Koreans. And I'm angry about that.

How can the government just let that happen? They could have done something. They could have, but they just stand back and let us kill each other off. So we have to solve it all ourselves. It's really difficult.

You know, it wasn't just the Rodney King verdict, it all built up with that Korean woman who had a liquor store and who shot that fifteen-year-old black girl. I think that, too, just built up all that anger and finally there was the [Rodney King] verdict and that triggered it. Then it all just went up.

I think that shooting was way too much. She had no right to kill that black girl. But you know, I used to help out when my parents had a liquor store in about the same area and there's a lot of kids who just come in and they're expert. They steal like crazy. You give them a chance, you sort of trust them, but they do it. And you have to understand, I guess, that no one taught them right from wrong. You have to understand that. But I bet it's scary for a Korean lady who probably can't really talk to them in English, so there's this language barrier, and probably she was really scared. I'm sure she was scared and she wasn't really thinking straight and she pulled the trigger.

I think it was way too much to shoot her, but I'm angry because there's been so many people with liquor stores getting killed. And the thing is, it's always a black person pretty much. We have so many cases where the blacks or the Mexicans shot the Korean person, but they never show that. The media, the public don't see that. They're always on the black side because they think they need more support, I guess.

Still, I feel closer to my black friends since the riots. I mean, I have no problem with blacks, I really don't. I think they're really good. I mean, they're like any other people. At my church there was a lot of blacks coming in or we'd go to black churches and try to break the barrier. So I guess we became a lot closer that way. This is the first time we're really actually trying to understand one another. I think it's good.

But for our family, I don't think we'll set up our store in the same place again because I think my parents would be too scared. Because of the racial tension. I mean, there's a lot of good ones, but there's still a lot of them who do not like Koreans, or the other way around. It's really difficult. I wish people would know that not all Koreans are prejudiced against blacks. I want people to understand that we're trying our best to relieve the tension. We're trying. We're trying to open up to blacks. It's hard because we were never opposed to them in the first place. I wish that we could be closer, but it's hard.

Quest looked very scary. I don't remember what his ethnic background was, but I guess that he was Hispanic, maybe black, I don't know. What was striking about him was that he was a Crip. That made me feel like right there a lot of things were going to be said, so I was real happy to interview him. I wasn't scared, and I wasn't not scared. I was right in the middle.

What made me not scared of him was that he's got to make a living, too. He's starting a new life, he told me, he wanted to change his life. He's studying real hard in school and he told me what college he's going to. After talking to him, I felt, damn, I don't know how they could be in a gang for so long and, just like snapping a finger, change their whole life. Start a new one. Become someone. Damn.

Eric Zamora, 16, Editor
with Rolando Liriano, 16, Editor

QUEST, 17

CE: So tell me about yourself, about your childhood. How was it?

QUEST: When I was growing up I saw a lot of activity, gang activities, people selling dope, you know, role models. I didn't want to be like them when I grew up. And now that I'm their age, I'm like them. I'm in a gang, gang-banging, out there shooting people, doing all type of crazy stuff.

CE: What are the reasons for shooting somebody?

QUEST: Well, when they come into my 'hood, they shoot one of my people, it's time to retaliate back.

CE: But for what reason?

QUEST: For their coming into the 'hood, shooting up my peoples, killing my peoples. Something had to be done. You can't let them slide like that.

CE: Tell me a little about how you first got into the gang. How old were you?

QUEST: I was thirteen when I first got into a gang. I started running the streets, started hanging with the homeboys, but I never really got initiated. I just had to prove myself. So I prove myself and here I am now.

CE: How did you prove yourself?

QUEST: By going out there, beating up people, the enemies, you know, shooting up and doing all type of stuff. Kicking back, smoking weed, doing this and doing that.

CE: And how did your parents feel about it?

QUEST: Well, my people never knew about it until I got locked up when I was fifteen.

CE: What did you do?

QUEST: I went in for second-degree murder. I did eighteen months.

CE: How was it like in jail?

QUEST: Well, it wasn't bad and it wasn't good. I just felt sad. Just thought I had to do my time and get out. That's it.

CE: Say any more about that?

QUEST: Nope.

CE: What do you think this community is missing? I mean, what does this community need?

QUEST: A lot more jobs out there. A lot more freedom. You know, you walk down the street, police stop you, for what, I don't know. No reason.

CE: Do you go to school?

QUEST: I go to Crenshaw. It's cool, you know, learn an education, meet new peoples, making right choices.

CE: I heard that the Crips and Bloods are planning to join up together.

QUEST: I think it's nonsense. It ain't real. If the Crips and the Bloods were peacing up, they would have peaced up a long time ago. It ain't real. It's not going to work. It's working right now in certain places, but you still got certain places out here that it ain't working. It's always going to be one person in the crowd that think they're harder than the next person, and they're going to start right back up there.

CE: What kinds of activities do you guys do?

QUEST: Gamble, go cruising, sell dope. Everything.

CE: How did you feel about the L.A. riots?

QUEST: I thought it was bad. I was locked up at the time, but to me, I felt like it was racist. I can't do nothing about it anyway. That wasn't my problem. I say the police is responsible. The police and the President. You know he come here, he said he was going to do something, but it ain't happening yet. They keep talking about it, but ain't nothing happening.

CE: What do you see for the future? For these gangs?

QUEST: Well, I just hope everything is calmed down. I'm planning to go to college, I want to live a good life, and I hope that this world will be better in the next ten years.

CE: What do you see for yourself in the future? What do you think you'll be doing?

QUEST: I want to be a probation officer, if it's possible, to work at a camp or something to relate to the kids that's growing up. When they get locked up, you know, I could relate to them because I've been through the same thing they've been through. Most people at the camps right now, they can't relate to these kids. But I'm living it right now, and later on, they'll need somebody to relate to. They need somebody to understand where they're coming from in order to get help.

We met Velma at a meeting in the school in Compton shortly after the L.A. riots. Compton was really creepy, with lots of funny little streets and houses with bars on all the windows. It seemed like the community lived totally in fear. Fear of gangs and gang reprisals.

This meeting was for parents to like cope with their kids being in gangs and living in a gang environment. There were only three parents there, and Velma was one of them. She was a sweetheart. I really liked her a lot and she had a lot of stuff to say. She was about forty-two. She was black. She was short. She was pudgy. She had three children, two younger ones and a sixteen-year-old daughter.

She said that eight people were murdered in her building in the past two years, and that really shocked me. She has so many plans for the future, if she can move away from Compton. I hope she can do what she wants to do. She's a great woman. She's very strong.

Hector Cruzado, 15, Editor

VELMA, 42

CE: What's it like raising your children up in Compton?

VELMA: Well, when they were younger, it was easier. Now that they're older and teenagers, their friends are into violence, into gangs, and it's kind of hard to try to keep them away from drugs and all when they're surrounded by it. It's really very difficult. I don't like it at all, but I can't afford to move right now, so I'm just stuck in the middle of it.

CE: How do you deal with problems that your daughters must face, like peer pressure, in school?

VELMA: Well, it's hard, and that's why I'm taking this parenting class, to try to get some help. I haven't had any serious problems so far, I've been lucky.

CE: Have you ever witnessed any gang-related violence?

VELMA: All the time. Yes. I live in a gang-violent apartment building. There's been eight murders in the building since we've been there, within the past two years. Right under our nose, our eyes.

CE: How does that make you feel?

VELMA: It feels terrible. It's just drive-bys, fights, stabbings. It's wild and senseless.

CE: So what can you do about the environment in your building?

VELMA: Well, I've been saving so we can move out before school starts again. I have family living in West Covina, so we're moving there. But I really don't think there's anyplace you can really go. I think violence is just everywhere. My mother just sent me a picture of a guy in West Covina at a taco stand just got killed. It's just ridiculous. There's no place that's safe anymore.

CE: How did you feel about the riots in Los Angeles?

VELMA: Well, I can't say I was for it. I'm not for stealing or violence, but I think it got a message across. It taught a lot of people a lesson that the blacks are serious. This prejudice is too much. But it shocked me. You were scared to move, you know.

CE: What do you feel about what happened to Reginald Denny?

VELMA: I think that was awful, unnecessary. It's just people striking out for no reason. They just don't know what else to do.

CE: I hear that since the riot, there's been a truce between the Crips and the Bloods. What do you think that means? Do you think it will last?

VELMA: I don't think it's going to last at all. I think they're just trying to make this riot die down and then they're going to start back. I think they enjoy it too much. You know, once you're used to killing people, you just can't stop.

CE: What do you think about the Los Angeles Police Department?

VELMA: I think it's the police's fault. I think the ones that beat Rodney King should be suspended or fired. They should start all over. And Chief Daryl Gates, him too, they should be rid of him. I can't stand him. He thinks black people are not human. All men are created equal but not to him.

It's because of him that the riot existed, you know. People are mad because the police are not doing nothing. It seem like they causing more problems than helping. I do not think he's the man for the job. No way.

CE: What do you think about Mayor Tom Bradley?

VELMA: I don't think he's doing anything either. He should be made to step down. I think they all need to be replaced. They need to start a new system or something.

CE: What about President Bush?

VELMA: The President, too. I don't like any of them. I don't even want to watch the news, I don't want to hear anything about them. It's all lies what they say, anyway. Once they get in office, they all lie. We should get *them* all vetoed!

Everywhere

———————————

In the back of the closet
Under the sink
behind the chair in the corner.
That's where the pain is.
Under the bed
Beside the stove
Inside the box in the basement.
That's where the addiction is.
Behind the curtain
Beneath the couch
Wedged between the magazines
That's where my life is.

KATHLEEN REHWALDT, 13

8

Hopeful Heroes

*I started getting locked up, getting beat up, getting robbed,
and I started realizing, Now I know how those people I
beat up feel, because I got beat up.*

MANNY, 20

*I want to see the little kids on my block grow up in a good
way. On the block today, the only chance you're gonna get
is the bad way.*

RICARDO, 16

*I'm living homeless by choice because out here there's more
love and there's more lookout for one another than anywhere I've ever seen in a family.*

REFUGIO, 20

Manny is a twenty-year-old who has been through hell and back and has the most phenomenally wonderful, positive attitude. He got himself off drugs by just telling himself that he wanted to live. He survived horrible physical abuse from the hands of his stepfather. Horrible. He's been in jail. He's been violent. He had guns. He's been stabbed. He had a drug addiction.

And now he's just making it by. He can't get a job, so he sells comic books on the street. This guy basically served as an inspiration to all of us. We gave him the microphone and he just went with it. He told a story and a half and he told a story of basically trials and tribulations and overcoming horrible negative odds. God bless him. I hope he's okay. He really just touched all of our hearts.

I keep thinking about Manny because he's been through so much, the kind of stuff I'd only seen in movies or heard about on television. But he's got this great attitude. He was really likable. A great guy, and he's floating around New York City somewhere. We don't even know if he's alive. It's really sad. No, sad doesn't cut it. Sad doesn't even begin to cover it.

Shane Tilston, 17, Editor

MANNY, 20, NEW YORK CITY

I guess I've known violence all my life, since I was about five or six when my stepfather started brutalizing me. I guess I did violence because that's all I knew. And drugs somehow seemed to make it better.

I grew up in Brooklyn. It's tough in Brooklyn. You have to be dressed hip and be down with everybody else, and if they get into a fight with a bunch of white kids, you have to get involved in it. You have to do stupid things like steal, rob, you know, all that crap, take drugs and things like that. I do admit it, when I was younger, I took drugs and hung out in a gang.

But then, as I grew older, I started learning that drugs and hanging out and being in gangs, it's not going to help me in life. It's not even gonna save my ass, 'cause in the streets, it's like . . . it's hectic. You know, the only way you could survive is to be yourself. Avoid problems. Avoid certain kinds of people you know that's gonna cause problems. Like if you see a certain group of kids hanging out, go around them. Don't go through them, 'cause if you go through them, you're going to get into serious trouble.

Right now, I'm trying to sell my Rollerblades for fifty bucks 'cause, well, it's hard to find a job. It's not easy finding jobs, especially if you ain't got a high-school diploma. I got kicked out of school in ninth grade—you know, too much fighting, carrying knives and guns and things like that to school. And I would pick fights to get kicked out of certain schools. I didn't want to be in that school. I even fought teachers. I fought a principal. I punched the principal in the mouth when I was young.

If I didn't fight, I wasn't satisfied. It was like a daily habit for me. And then I hit seventeen and I got locked up for a year because of fighting and assault charges and things like that. Came out, started learning, you know, jail is not the place, streets is not the place. The only place that it can be is through yourself, in your heart.

Now I'm drug-free. I just did it with willpower because I was realizing it was killing me and I was wasting too much money on drugs. I would spend two to three hundred dollars a day taking cocaine and smoking pot. That shit almost killed me. The only drug I take now is smoking cigarettes and drinking coffee. That's caffeine and nicotine. It's still bad, but it's a slow death.

I basically raised myself in the streets 'cause my mother wasn't there for me. She was home, but she wasn't there. She could be in the living room, I could walk into the house, and she wasn't there. She would not treat me like I was there, you know? She literally threw me out when I was younger so her boyfriend could live there.

And my stepfather, he used to beat me. He used to make me bend over the bed, naked, and beat me with a leather belt until I bled. Now, that's kinda crazy, you know what I mean? He used to do that to me and my brother, and then he would tell us if we did good in school he would buy us something, like clothes. We'd do good in school, and he wouldn't buy us shit.

He'd leave us without buying anything. We were kids with no clothes, nothing.

So me and my brother started doing stuff to make money and live. We started stealing, 'cause that was the only way of survival. And then my mom and my stepfather would say that we were no good and all this and that and I said, If you would have helped us when we was younger, we wouldn't have been in this area where we are now.

They said, Oh, we did everything for you, we did this and we did that, and then they would send me to a psychiatrist. I tell the psychiatrist what they did to me and he would ask my parents if it was true and they would deny it and then when I got home I'd get beat again. Then I would go to school with beat marks and my parents would say I fell down the stairs—you know, that old line—so in other words, I was child-abused.

I turned rebellious against them at the age of fourteen and that's when I started hanging out in the streets and doing all this other shit because nobody will help me. I would do good in school, hoping I'd get something. But I would never get anything, so I said, Fuck it. I'm not going to go to school if I'm not gonna get nothin' for it, you know what I mean? I didn't realize how much I needed school.

I was living in the streets for a while, but then I said, That's not gonna help me. I said, Let me go home. 'Cause I was hungry, I'd go into the house when my mother wasn't there and steal food and take my bath, wash myself, change, and then go back in the streets. Every day I would do that and then I started stealing money from them. I stole two hundred dollars from my grandmother 'cause nobody would buy me toys, and I played with the money, but then I gave it all away to my friends because I couldn't take it home.

You know, a lot of these kids have broken lives. They don't have nobody to take care of them. They don't have nobody helping them. They have to do it all their life, practically helping themselves. Some of them came from good families and they're still fucked up. Me, I came from a bad family and I'm fucked up, anyway.

Now, basically, I'm a collector. I collect comics, I buy things and then sell them. Just to survive, I sell my comics. I keep them or make trade-offs. Like I give someone a bunch of comics that's worth three dollars and they'll give me a comic that's worth twenty dollars and I'll sell it for fifteen or ten dollars, and that way I can get a profit. That's a way of living, you know, you gotta survive that way.

You come out here every day, you're going to see how crazy it is. And how hard these people work just to survive. In a way it's good, 'cause we learn, we learn experience 'cause we're in the street and you learn from the streets, you learn to survive. Like some homebound kids, they're in the house, they don't know much about the streets. If you left them out in the streets for about a week without a place to live, they'd probably go crazy. They wouldn't know how to survive.

You know, you tell somebody something, they don't learn their lesson until they see it happen to themselves. Like when my big brother used to tell me, Don't take drugs anymore, man. Chill out with it, don't do this shit anymore. I didn't want to listen to him, I was like, You did it for so many years, man, you're gonna tell me now not to do it? But then I started getting locked up, getting beat up, getting robbed, and I started realizing, Now I know how those people that I beat up feel, because I got beat up. I started realizing a lot of shit because what I did to people, they did to me. They say what goes around comes around and, I might say, it came around to me.

So, right at this moment, I just try to survive. Later on in the future, I don't know what's going to happen to me. For what I know, I could be dead tomorrow. But I'm really going to try to straighten out my life, try to make it somewhere. I'd like to get a high-school diploma, but I can't right now because I really don't have a stable environment. I have a permanent address but not a permanent residence.

I try to live day by day now. Buy my comics, read my comics, then sell them. If I die, at least I died reading my comics, you know, I did something I enjoy.

211

Ricardo and his friends and people in their neighborhood all live a life of fear. They're all afraid that they're going to get shot. It's very common for them to have, if not a gun, some sort of weapon on them at all times for protection.

Ricardo is Dominican. He was sixteen when I interviewed him and he's very nice. He was very easy to interview. He just went on and on about everything and anything under the sun that had to do with his life.

He made me have a lot of respect for him. He was very honest. He told me that his neighborhood gets very violent; there's always trouble going on. He doesn't like it there, but his mother can't afford to move and anyway, he said, he could never turn his back on his neighborhood.

After the interview I felt a big hole in me, like something bad had just happened. Because Ricardo made me feel like I was a part of his life. When he would tell a story, I'd feel like I was just standing there. I felt like I was there when his friend Hector was hit with the gun handle.

You know, when you live in New York, you know all this happens, you know that there's violence everywhere. You know that kids are running around with guns and you don't know why unless you're one of them or unless you happen to be lucky enough to talk to them and figure it all out. For people who don't live in New York and don't live in big cities, they don't see this, but they still need to know that it's out there.

All of us who have worked on this book have learned a lot, a lot more than we thought we'd learn. I hope Ricardo takes this experience and can help other kids. When he gets older and he's not a kid anymore, he can remember what his childhood was like and maybe he can make a difference for other people.

Sarah Young, 17, Editor

RICARDO, 16, BROOKLYN

I'm sixteen years old and I'm Spanish. I'm Dominican. I like to rap and stuff like that. I like to dance, too. I live in Brooklyn and it's kind of a rough neighborhood there, where I live.

Out there where I live, they sell a lot of drugs. They have a lot of guns out there. You don't want to get involved with it. I used to be scared, but now I'm not scared because I know how the whole thing goes. It's like, they done it so many times, it's like, forget about it, whatever happens, happen. To me it doesn't matter, it's like, I'm eating and watching TV and it's like somebody shoots, it's like wow. It's like a firecracker, so I'm not going to pay attention to it. That's how it is out there where I live.

They shoot each other just to have fun, you know. It's like it's going crazy. Our block is crazy. I don't have a gun now, but I used to carry weapons, like knives, kitchen knives that could really cut. Like a meat cleaver or something like that. I did it to protect myself in case anything happens, you know. Like if anything goes down, if anybody tries to rob me or something, it's just right there and I could pull it out. Because it's all by respect, you know.

It's not like you can just walk down the street. In my block if you get beat up you're a pussy, man, you're like the lowest. You do not belong on that block. So that's why you have to have your respect, so nobody will mess with you. And the way you get respect is if you go out there and you fight other people on their block, you get respect there and then. They'll hear about you and then it's like, once you have all that respect, people are going to see that you know what's up, you're big like them, they ain't gonna mess with you. That's the way it goes. That's the biggest thing in the streets, to have your respect.

Around my building it's very dangerous. Very, very dangerous. And I don't live in no projects, I live in an apartment and halfway down my block is houses. In my building there's a basement and a lot of crackheads go down there to smoke. And then a lot of them come and deal down there and say, Yo, where's my money? If I don't get my money by tomorrow, you're gonna get shot.

And it really happens, you know, it really happens, especially on my roof. On my roof it's like, there's a lot of gunshots, *pow, pow, pow,* you hear like five of them, or six. You know, just flying up in the air, you can even hear the bullets going *zzziiirrr*, zoom away. In the middle of the night.

In the daytime, there's only drug addicts and stuff like that. There's hardly any fights. So I hang out. But after twelve I go to my house because I know something's always gonna happen. At night, it's hell, man. It's fuckin' hell.

I know I cannot live in a good neighborhood because my mother doesn't have the money to move into a good neighborhood, so I have to just keep on living where I live at. It's like that's my place. That's my home. That's everything. That neighborhood means everything to me. It's like a friend, it's like my best friend. Even though there's a lot of fights, it's still like my best friend.

To tell you the truth, I think this violence is going to keep on like this for a long time. Because cops can't even stop crime today. They be gettin' shot, too. They're afraid, too. They're afraid of what's going to happen to them 'cause they hardly even want to get involved with gun shooting around them, you know, 'cause like it's too much. It's too much crime out there.

The only way you could stop violence is if you start bringing some robots out there and some transformers. If you try to stop a fight between human beings, definitely something's going to happen to you, man. Definitely.

There's no way to resolve these things without fighting. There is no way. You'll never solve these things, you know, because it's so hard for people. You try to talk to somebody, like let's say he started with you, like, Why you have to push for, man? It'll be like, Yo, man, I pushed you because I don't li— Come on, please man, yo, just chill out man, just chill out. Chill out? Chill this, man! *Pow!* And he'll hit you right in the face, and you're gonna fight back. You can never solve it.

You may want to try, to say, Come on, give me that handshake. But then, right there, you lost your respect. You lost your whole respect, because then they'll give you like, Damn, man, I smashed him on the face and this punk, man, he's trying to befriend me. Get the hell out of here, man. Watch him when he comes down the block, watch what a beating I'm gonna give this punk, man. You see, you cannot solve this, you cannot just talk it out. It's so hard to do that. Can't do that. It's too hard. Especially now.

Now, I don't have a gun. But sometimes, sometimes I carry like a little weapon, just in case something happens. Because, you know, they always try to pick on little kids, and I'm sixteen but I look like a little kid, and it's like, Damn, he's just a little fuckin' asshole, you know. So they'll try to pull out something and if they pull out something, then I'm going to pull out something, too. And that's how I'm going to get my respect.

But I'm also doing good in my grades. I never cut out, I always go to school, man, because I want to be something in life. I want to be an architect. That's my dream. And, you know, now I'm trying to help other kids, too, help them see they can be somebody if they try. So I'm going to keep on doing good because I want to go to college. I want to be something.

Then, when I've graduated and all, I'll go back to my neighborhood. I mean, if I'm rich, right, I'll go back and help them out. If I have enough money to support myself, then I'm going to support half my block. I'm going to support my friends and see how they're doing.

I want to see the little kids on my block grow up in a good way, and not in a bad way. On the block today, the only chance you're gonna get is the bad way. But maybe I can get through college and come back and make the bad road better. That's my dream, anyway.

Refugio was a squatter, which means that he was homeless, but he had a condemned building that he and some other people fixed up. He knew everybody in Golden Gate Park. He was real outgoing and he had a great attitude about people. He loved people.

If you knew his background, you would wonder how he could have so much trust and love for other people, because he was so abused by life and society. He was a crack addict, but he got himself off crack. He didn't eat regularly because he was homeless pretty much.

He was a philosopher. He gave people advice and they, in turn, would help him out. This is how Refugio feels he is needed. He knows all of the homeless teenagers, he knows all of their stories. He's Mexican, and he even knows the skinheads, who probably don't think too kindly of him because of the color of his skin, but Refugio seems to just have love for them, too.

We owe a lot to Refugio for making our San Francisco trip really positive and eventful. We got close to him because he shared a lot of his pain with us and we cared about him. We would bring him food at night and we cared about him. It was very difficult to say good-bye to him.

You know, you wonder if you're ever going to see these people again. Probably not. But they're really our heroes. All the kids who talked to us are the heroes of this book.

Shane Tilston, 17
Sarah Young, 17
Editors

REFUGIO, 20, SAN FRANCISCO

My name is Refugio Resugio. Resugio is Spanish, meaning savior, so they tell me. I was pretty much a mama's boy; I didn't know my dad too much. He was basically the type of person that would come in the house, stay for a couple of days, and then go someplace else for another couple of months. My dad was a wonderful person, but he had a little bit of the adventure boy in him, you know. He didn't want to be tied down with responsibility and stuff.

I didn't understand much when I was a kid and I didn't like

that my dad wouldn't take me to the baseball game or the football game or just teach me how to fight and do all that other stuff. So I guess what I got mostly as a child was emotional abuse.

When I started going to school I was at the top of my class. I was in the top ten in the spelling bee in second grade. Then I started turning in the fourth grade and things started dropping. I just started daydreaming and other kids would pick on me because I was such a small little kid and so I had more emotional abuse at school.

By the time I got into the sixth grade, I was totally rebellious. I wanted to do everything that nobody wanted to do. Everything that was bad for me I did. The only good quality that I had in the sixth grade was that I listened to everybody's problems. I would open my heart to them, but then a lot of people could hurt me that way.

By ninth grade, I don't remember much because I was into my ditching stage. I wanted to do everything that everybody else was doing. I was a follower. By that time I was also interested in girls, but I was a scrawny little thing, so not very many girls would like me very much.

By that time my parents and everybody else said, Uh-oh, this guy's going downhill fast. And I was like, What's wrong with me? What's going on? Every time I tried to do something good, to fight back, somebody would talk down to me and I'd go back downhill further. I was feeling totally bad, totally depressed, totally sorry for myself.

Then I started getting into swimming. Me and my friends used to jump over the fence to the Roosevelt swimming pool because it's outside and we used to go skinny-dipping in there at about three in the morning. In the middle of the city. It was cool. We used to get up on the high dives butt-naked and just jump into the water and stuff. And then I looked like I had a cold or something, I kept sniffling and so my mom thought I was doing cocaine. I couldn't exactly say, No, Mom, I'm going skinny-dipping at Roosevelt. So I just tried to hide it and she thought I was a drug addict.

By the time I got to the eleventh grade, I wanted to quit school. Everything about teachers I hated. I hated everything about teachers because they forced work upon you and wouldn't give you space to say, Hey, I need your help. They didn't want to help you. So I just said, No thank you, I don't want to do that anymore, and I quit school.

And then I started getting into crack. One of my friends, who I thought was a friend, told me to try some and gave it to me. This is a peer-pressure drug. I did not want to try it for fear of what might happen and, sure enough, it messed me up. It messed me up real bad for seven months.

I would hang out in crack houses, I used to not change for three weeks. I smelled really bad. I did not care about my hygiene. I was into the dealing business, I used to deal into the thousands, and every single profit I ever made I smoked it. I smoked about three hundred dollars a day worth of crack. I stood out in the middle of the night wondering if I was going to get a knife in my back. I lost a lot of my mentality.

I didn't want anything to do with anything. Nothing to do with my family. I ripped my family off. I ripped off cars. Me and my friends could strip cars down to the frame alone in fifteen minutes. Everything, engine and all. I was a sad subject.

Finally, after seven months, I got off it. I did it on willpower. But I went through the worst withdrawal you can imagine. For like a month, a whole entire month of nothing but cold fevers, sweating in the nighttime, going to the bathroom, looking at myself in the mirror and crying, saying, I need it, I want it. I have dreams where I can hear it calling to me.

But it's so bad, it makes you lose a dramatic amount of weight, it turns your brain cells into water. I've seen too many people go down on that drug. It's a bad drug and I don't think anybody should do it.

Recently I moved out to this park. I started finding out that people here rely on trading for everything. They don't rely on money. Some people say you can't have any pleasure if you don't have money, right? I don't believe that. I believe if you believe in nature, you believe in God. If you believe in doing the things that you want to do for your own satisfaction, you can do it.

I get a little money when I need it. I get my money by giving other people advice. I told this one guy who was panhandling out here the other day, I told him, Why don't you just get a shopping cart and go out in the middle of the night and pick up cans? The guy goes out, he made himself fifty dollars in one day and gave me ten dollars. That's my commission that I get for giving good advice.

There's an organization that's been coming out every week for years and years to feed people and the cops tried to bust those guys. They tried to bust them and throw them in jail for feeding the homeless. I thought that was a really ignorant thing, so I told them, Hey, don't fight back physically, organize! So they got organized and they got a petition and they got all the homeless to sign it, giving their consent to be fed, and they went to the courts and now the police cannot touch them. They cannot touch them and that's what I call a cool thing.

You know, I can even give yuppies advice. Yuppies are considered people who wear suits, go on an eight-hour-a-day job, struggle to make their life happen so that they can earn the things that they want and still be unhappy. I could tell them about nature and God and stuff, and they might not be so unhappy all the time.

I would like other people to understand that there's a lot of other people out here who talk people down and call them bums, call them all these other different things, and it really hurts them really bad. I see homeless people every day who cry, who suffer, who get talked down so much to where they even think about committing suicide.

I think there are too many men into building cities and atom bombs and things. I say, Chill out, all you construction workers, why not do your construction for building trees and parks and playgrounds for children who need them?

It hurts to see that mankind can actually have the power to

think up things like the atomic bomb, you know. It's really stupid. To think of something that's going to destroy life on Earth. All you're going to see is a bunch of souls going nowhere, living in pain for that one moment just to go, Whoa, yo! My life is over.

Kids are the most important thing there is. They're very interesting and very innocent. I want to have plenty of kids of my own. I think I'll go for the world record of fifty-three. I want kids so bad because there's that personal satisfaction of going through the heartache of teaching them how to do things that you know they want to learn and you want them to learn.

Like racism, for instance. To me racism doesn't start by a person saying, Hey, I was born white, so I think I should hate black people. No, it's not like that. You grow to be a racist, you are taught to be a racist by what your parents do or say. So I want to teach my kids that you don't have to be stereotyped to somebody. There are all kinds of different people out there and there are many who are very cool. There are people out there who are different than you and who you can still have as a best friend. But don't be too gullible, either, you know. This is the time when it's going to get really, really bad. Be careful.

I'm living homeless by choice. I'm living homeless by choice because out here there's more love and there's more lookout for one another than anywhere I've ever seen in a family. Out here is the place where my heart is. This is what I call home. Because I have other people looking out for me. I have friends who I can actually hug. I have friends who come up to me and say, Hey, I love you.

9

Epilogue: Can We Create a Better Future to Give Back to Our Children?

How did your experience interviewing for this book affect your thinking about violence in America? Did it change you in any way?

MICHELLE: Doing the book has brought it alive, violence. It's not just people on TV.

RANDY: It brought it alive in the sense that I used to walk down the street in my neighborhood and see it, but I'd be too scared to look at somebody and say, How did that affect you? How did that punch in the face make you feel? You're talking to these kids and they told you how it made them feel.

AMY: It made it easier for me to talk to people, especially people I'm usually uncomfortable with. The very first interview I did was with three guys, all by myself, and it was the scariest thing I'd ever done. But I learned that even though someone is

221

violent, or they've been in trouble before, they're not always a bad person.

TJ: My stereotypes were completely shattered. I had never experienced anything like the violence we heard about, or imagined that anyone could. When you are a child, you are supposed to do silly little things. These kids were talking about things that I know I will probably never experience in my life. It's hard to grasp that concept.

It also made me more connected with people. Not necessarily understanding their position or what kind of situation they're in, but just being able to recognize that they're there, and to be in touch with them. Not feel sorry for them, but kind of understand a little.

CHANDA: I've learned not to judge people and not to stereotype them. I learned that all these kids I talked to are the same as I am. Before I had done the interviews, I would have been scared of some of the people I talked to, because I didn't understand them. I hadn't really ever talked to people like that.

And then I went into these detention centers and talked to gang members and I got a totally different perspective. It's like I learned they had feelings and the same fears that I did. They have dreams, they have hopes, they've had disappointments. They have all these feelings that I have.

ROBIN: It made me realize how oblivious I was to all the violence that's going on. I mean, I'd see it in the news and read it in the paper, but it would just be another statistic and I wouldn't really identify with it, almost blocked it out of my mind. But after doing the interviews, I can place a face with the statistics and then it really starts to affect you.

SARAH: Yeah, it was very upsetting to me because in New York, of course, there's at least one murder, one robbery, one rape, one something happening to somebody every day. But you don't know the people and so you just let it go by. Then, when you find out, when you actually talk to kids your age or younger and their parents beat them or they have guns or they go to school where they have metal detectors 'cause everyone has a gun or knives— when you talk to people that horrible things are actually happening to, then it gets to be a part of your life. So I guess it was a good experience for me, but it was also very upsetting to discover that there is so much violence in our society. Something really needs to be done or else no one's going to be left. I don't know what to do about it, but we have to do something.

SHANE: Growing up in New York City, there's always stuff about violence on the news. You walk down the street and see people lying in gutters and you learn to look away. It's just much easier to pretend they're not there. But after you talk to them, after you talk to just a few people in that situation, you learn that everyone has their own story. They're not all hobo bums who just drank their way there or something. Everyone has a reason. So now, when I'm walking down the street and I see someone sleeping there or something, I think more about it. I try to wonder what brought them there. I can't just walk by anymore. But I don't know what to do either. I want to do something to help each and every one of them, but I don't know what to do. It's hard.

KATE: I talked to two different kinds of people during the interviews. One type of person was the victim—people whose lives were hurt by crime. They don't want our pity. They want our help to end the crime problem and to stop this violence, but they don't want us to just sit there and cry for them. That's not going to do anybody any good.

The other group that I talked to was the people in the juvenile detention center, the people who were actually committing acts of violence. I realized that I can't understand why they're doing it, but I don't have to understand it. I learned that when I talked to them there was no way I could ever comprehend why they did this stuff, but I could still talk to them and I didn't necessarily have to fear them. That was really important to me.

KATHLEEN: The interviewing process made me become more sensitive to the plight of children who face violence in their everyday lives, and what a tragedy it is that children, of all people, children who have done nothing, are victims of abuse and crime. It's also a tragedy that young people sometimes even feel like they have to commit crimes just for survival or acceptance in a gang because they don't have a family.

I discovered how the environment can shape somebody. A lot of the people we interviewed are like me, but their environment is different, their home life is different, the friends they hang around with are different, and they get involved with crime. So many young lives are ruined by violence. I wasn't aware of that before.

KATE: I think the most frustrating thing about the experience is that I'm more aware now, I know more about the violence that's happening, but I don't know what to do. When I talked to the kids at the juvenile detention center, my heart totally went out to them, and I really felt that they were victims of their environment. But I had no idea how to help or what to do next.

WENDY: Everybody we talked to had this awful story of someone beating them or somebody bad at school or somebody with drugs. Even the kids who were from affluent families had terrible stories to tell. It's scary when the person who does not experience violence is in the minority.

CAT: There's no way that I could have been in a situation where I would have learned so much about people who are so different from me. I wouldn't have ever known the people that I was interviewing if it hadn't been for this book. It was incredible to me that the things that they were saying had actually happened to them. And you were right there looking at the person that it happened to. Usually the stories that a person has gone through, like their whole history, are wrapped inside their body. So even if you see them walking down the street or sit next to them in math class, you don't know what's happened to them. It was like the stories of their lives were just coming out. It was really powerful.

How did the experience affect your attitudes?

SARAH: Some of the people we interviewed really terrified me. People in San Francisco scared me. I knew that they weren't going to hurt me after a while, but I also knew that they knew that I am the most opposite person from them that you can be.

Other people I felt very sorry for. My heart went out for them and I wanted to help them, like Manny and some of the others. It made me angry that they were in that situation.

WENDY: When we were at Boys School, one of the guys told me they were just as afraid of coming to my neighborhood, where it's mostly white, mostly upper class, as I was going to their neighborhood, which is inner city with a lot of ethnic minorities. If they were walking down my street, what could happen was just as uncertain as what would happen if I was walking down their street. You never really think about that flip side of things. I think it's no big deal walking down my street because it's relatively crime-free, but for them, they don't know if someone could come out of their house and make racial slurs at them and they'd be just as scared as I would be where people carry guns.

AMY: My mom's always telling me to lock the door and don't drive downtown alone at night and all like that. After the interviews for the book, I remember coming home one day and I said, Mom, they're people. Yeah, there are problems out there, and yeah, there's violence, but you can't hide from everyone and never talk to someone because you think they may be violent. You have to talk to people. I'm not saying I want to go out and make all my new friends gang members, but I don't think it's a bad thing to be a friend to someone who's had a rough experience or who is going to be a violent person. You don't have to get involved in their life totally, but it's not bad to talk to that person and be a friend.

CHANDA: I think talking to someone is what you need to do because in my school—I live in an all-white county, we have two blacks in my county—people in my school are so oblivious to things such as violence and dealing with other races. There are people in my school that are so racist—like they'll say, I hate blacks. I go, Have you ever talked to one or met one? And they'll say, No, but I watch the news. [Laughs]

You've got to talk to people. If you don't talk to them, then you're just as bad as anyone who commits a crime, because you're committing a crime by judging someone unfairly. The biggest thing I learned was the importance of talking to people and trying to get the story behind their actions.

KATHLEEN: The interviews really changed my attitude because I think otherwise I would have grown up to be a typical adult. I would have totally not cared about children's issues or the problems children are facing in their lives if I hadn't had this experience. A lot of people forget what it's like to be a kid, to be a minority, to have people not care about you, to have the government spend less money on you, to not have the right to vote. I think a lot of people tend to forget that. Since I've had this experience, I will never forget what it's like to be a kid. I want to be an advocate for children.

KATE: The first thing interviewing for this book taught me is what my beliefs might actually be. One day my mom was driving me to Children's Express for an interview and I mentioned that we were going to the juvenile detention center. She said, Why are you going there? Why are you going to talk to the scum of society? Why is CE forcing you to do this? [Laughs] And I thought, Wow, we grow up with the beliefs of our parents, they are ingrained in our minds. I wondered if I really thought these people were the scum of society. Is this how I believe? Is this how I've treated these people?

Then I talked to them and I realized they're not worse than me, they're not inferior to me. Even though one of the people in my interview group was a murderer, I don't think that he's less than me. I don't approve of his actions. But it's just— My mom just totally surprised me. It made me wonder if I felt like she does. I don't think so.

AMY: It's like with disabled people. We're taught to look the other way, don't stare, pretend they're not there. People look the other way with violence, too, especially in the inner cities. But it happens every day. Shootings happen every day in Indianapolis and half the time you don't even hear about them. You hear about the suburban gang fight in school, or a little fight between students or something. You never hear about the nightly shootings in poor neighborhoods. It's gotten so bad that people are just turning away from it. They feel so hopeless, they just ignore it.

WENDY: And when people look the other way, the problems don't get addressed and it just gets worse. Nobody wants to take responsibility to help fix it, but people are crying out for help and nobody hears it. They go about their business and don't even stop and look.

So maybe with this book people will stop and look and really *see* into the lives of people who are crying out for help. I hope it will make some people think twice about kids who need help.

Do you think, if more people had the experience you've had doing the book, and the understanding you have after talking with these people, that things would be any different from the way they are now?

SARAH: It's nice to pretend, but no matter what you do, there's always going to be people who don't agree or who feel it's okay to beat children. There's always going to be people who drag their kids down the street crying and don't help them. There's always going to be people who take drugs and who need to steal and rob people and kill them so that they can have money to take their drugs.

The people who worked on this book were excited to do it, we wanted to do it, even though we didn't know what to expect. We didn't know who we were going to meet, and when we did, it was very emotional. It was very draining. But we did it and it was a great experience, though I don't think it's for everybody. I think what we did was unique. I don't think that it could be something everyone could do to learn about violence.

MICHELLE: I don't suppose we're telling people anything that they don't already know about violence. They know violence is there. But I think what we're saying to them is how severe it is and how young it's starting with kids.

SHANE: Violence isn't real to most people. If you see it on television enough and you see it in the movies enough, see enough people get shot that way, then you don't really see someone getting shot anymore. It sort of washes over you. And then you have little kids, with their toys and stuff, killing each other. They kill somebody and he'll be dead for ten seconds and then he'll come and sneak up behind the other guy and shoot him. So none of it's real, it's all fantasy.

SARAH: If you see enough violent movies, you know the person didn't really die 'cause you're going to see him in the sequel, in the next movie. You know on TV if someone gets shot, they didn't die because the show has to continue for the rest of the season. In cartoons, they never die. They can walk off cliffs and they're still walking. It's not real. But the violence that *is* real is going on in our streets and in our cities and everywhere, and a lot of people do see it. I even think the ones who don't see it know what's out there. They just can't relate to it in any way.

They haven't talked to people who've experienced it. They can't possibly have a clue how tough life is out there.

Do you think your talking with these kids and their being able to tell you their story was helpful to them?

SARAH: Some of the kids that I interviewed, I could tell, really wanted to talk. They had so much to say, they just wanted to pour out their whole life story and they wanted someone to listen to them.

Some of them were actually living on the street and they had no one to take care of them, no one to help them. It's funny, the kids we talked to who were in institutions or in bureaucratic organizations weren't as talkative and weren't as interested in the book. But once they got started talking, then they just wanted to tell you everything, too.

SHANE: A lot of the kids we talked to are in the position they're in because they've been ignored by their parents. So they feel really great when someone actually wants to sit down and listen to them. Just the fact that someone cared enough to sit and talk with them really meant something to them. One guy actually came up to me afterward and thanked me for letting him just talk. That really gave me a good feeling, like I was actually able to do something and not just walk in and take something, take his story, and then leave.

WENDY: I think that it gives them a second perspective, because if they experience violence all the time, then they might think that it's the only way to live because that's all they see. But then when we talked with them, they might see that living from day to day and listening to gunshots and walking past gangs on the way to school isn't how everybody lives in this country. There are people who go to school where there is not a whole lot of violence or don't have to come home and have nobody at home. There are people who can come home and find food in the refrigerator.

229

RANDY: I think our talking with them made a difference to those kids at Boys Center. They could sit down and share their feelings with me. I think it made a difference to them and it definitely made a difference to me. It just made me feel good that I could tell these kids that you don't have to listen to what these people say about being a sissy. You're a human being, you have feelings, you cry, you laugh, you do all that. That's what it's all about—violence, laughing some, crying definitely—and they just didn't have a chance to do that.

KATHLEEN: I think a lot of the kids were actually surprised, like they would turn the tables on us and ask *us* questions. They were surprised to hear that I hadn't ever seen a gang except in the movies or on TV.

ROBIN: I felt that they realized they were never going to see us again. We'd walk in and then we'd walk out and our job was done. Because we would never see them again almost gave them some bonding between us and they could feel comfortable talking with us. They were as shocked at our life as we were at their life, which is incredibly upsetting.

CHANDA: I don't think it was so much telling their stories that might have made a difference as that someone cared. I think it was just someone wanting to talk with them that meant a lot to them.

KATHLEEN: For me it was weird to see kids that had so many worries. When I was a kid, I liked watching cartoons, I liked riding my Big Wheel and playing Star Wars. They have to worry about being safe and being inside. It was just so weird. I think a lot of American people have the impression that childhood is carefree, that it's innocent, but for a lot of people it's really not.

Adults always talk about how much worse the youth of today are. Do you think that kids today are worse off than kids fifty or twenty years ago?

TJ: I think compared to twenty years ago, today is definitely worse than it was. Years ago they probably didn't have crack, or at least not as much as there is today. And the weapons are becoming more sophisticated. Now they have automatic machine guns.

CHANDA: There's so many things going on that maybe some of these kids feel suffocated, like they're in a whirlwind, they're in a cyclone and they can't get out. Their frustration leads to murdering someone or robbing a store or something, and they can't deal with it.

WENDY: There's always going to be some violence. There was some violence twenty years ago, there was violence fifty years ago, but when violence starts to take over, it's a scary thing.

AMY: To have to worry about their older brothers or worry about being in a gang when they grow up and getting into that crowd . . . I can't imagine thinking about that stuff when I was that young. Childhood isn't supposed to be like that.

CHANDA: They wanted to do little-kid things, but because of their neighborhood, they couldn't. They wanted to be kids, but something was preventing them from doing that. They didn't know how to deal with that, other than being violent. They didn't know any alternative.

KATHLEEN: It's like there's no longer a childhood, like the time span for childhood is just shrinking for kids. Some of the things they come in contact with just blew my mind. They came in contact with alcohol at nine and ten years old. I used to think it was so wonderful that when you're a child you're naive and oblivious to all these problems, you're carefree. It's all just shrinking and some people don't have it at all. It's very sad. Those kids are just so incredibly resilient to the violence. The younger ones, they didn't dwell on it. They just accepted it as part of their life. It's there and it happens, but they don't dwell on it.

231

WENDY: You have to be resilient. If you let all that get to you day after day after day, you'd totally have a nervous breakdown. If you think about it too much, if you think about your block being infested with cocaine addicts and drug dealers and gunshots and gangs, that's a lot to handle, especially for a kid that's seven or eight or nine years old. So you always have to look for the flowers and the trees and stuff like that if you're going to survive.

KATHLEEN: Another thing that I learned from the book is that the system doesn't work. I learned that at Girls School. These girls were not bad people. They lived in bad environments and, to get away from that, they would commit a crime. Then they were guaranteed to go to Girls School, have a bed, have a warm place to live, have hot meals. They were guaranteed that and they didn't get that at home.

What has society become when there are children that prefer to be living locked up because it's safer there than out on the streets? Being locked up is no longer a deterrent to crime, it's an incentive to get arrested. I met people that described Girls School as being a wonderland. Something's very wrong here.

AMY: Crime has gotten sort of appealing. If you do get a real honest job—like at McDonald's, if you dropped out of school— you can make fifty or seventy-five dollars a week. Or you can go and deal drugs and make a thousand dollars a day, have a nice car, have whatever you want. What are you going to do? I think if I was in that situation and I knew that I couldn't go to college 'cause I didn't have the education and I had no other opportunities, I'd probably deal drugs, too. The incentive is there to do crime. Kids aren't offered anything else.

KATE: Some kids aren't ever taught that it's wrong to hit someone or wrong to do drugs. Their parents do it, so why not? If you're never taught that, how are you going to know? It's awful that some people don't even know what's right and wrong.

232

They think all this violence is cool—a fun thing to go out and do on a Saturday night or any night.

CHANDA: I think we live in a very hypocritical society. I mean, you cannot even watch a cartoon on TV anymore that doesn't have some form of violence in it. Stuff that we grew up watching, like Tom and Jerry and Casper the Friendly Ghost, they're so violent. And then you go to school and you have all these people telling you that it's wrong to hit someone, it's wrong to do drugs and everything. And you're like, Well then, why is everyone doing it? Your life is filled with violence in all directions, even if you live in suburbia.

What kind of feeling did the interviews leave you with?

AMY: The day I went to the juvenile center, I went home that night and I cried. I just cried 'cause I felt so guilty. I mean, I wake up every morning. I don't wake up in the middle of the night to the sound of gunshots. I can't imagine what that would be like, just living in that kind of fear, or having my other brother be in a gang and worrying about him all the time, or worrying about my parents. I just can't imagine that. And I want to understand so bad. But you just can't understand unless you've been there.

KATHLEEN: I felt really thankful and really fortunate, and I finally was able to appreciate what I really had. I've had the opportunity to have a safe childhood. I go to a school where I feel safe, I've had a good education and people that supported me and role models. Just so many more opportunities than the people we interviewed have had. So many people don't have hope. I'm just thankful that I have hope.

TJ: I went out from most interviews feeling very frustrated because I wanted to do something, I wanted to help them, but I didn't know how. Then the feeling kind of changed to feeling

233

sad and depressed because I knew that there wasn't really anything that I could do to drastically change their lives.

CHANDA: Like TJ, the biggest feeling I had was frustration because there was nothing that I could do. I knew that I was doing something by helping to produce this book, but I just felt like it wasn't enough. It wasn't half as much as what I wanted to do. I wanted to bring home some of those kids, have them stay with me, but I couldn't.

SARAH: I realized that my life wasn't as bad as I sometimes thought it was. I learned that I am one of the lucky ones. I've never been beaten by my parents, I've never been in a place where I saw someone's head get shot off. When I was growing up, I thought everybody's life was like mine. But it isn't. And what's interesting is that the kids we interviewed think everybody's life is like *theirs.* So we're all wrong.

WENDY: I find myself wondering, Where are those kids now? Are they still alive, even? Some of them were living day to day, not knowing if there was food in the refrigerator or if they would be shot in the street on their way to school. They were real people. They're more than just voices in a book. They're people that are walking around the streets somewhere in Texas or Indiana or New York or wherever.

Do you think there's any hope for kids and teenagers in America in the future?

AMY: When I talked to those kids, they didn't know that they could do things with their lives. No one ever told them, You can make good grades, you can go to college, or you can *be* anything. Their parents could care less that they quit school or that they come home and smoke pot, or not go to school at all. It is so sad, all those parents who just don't care.

234

SARAH: Without parents to support kids, they have no one to go to. So they look up at the people who are in gangs, and then they get in the gang and then they have to sell drugs because that's their job in the gang, and they have to steal cars and they have to do all this stuff. It takes like ten years and then they wonder, Why am I doing this? I did it because I needed someone to help me. I needed friends. And then they realize, by the time they're twenty-five, I want to go back. I want to get my GED. I want to get a job. But there are no jobs for people who haven't been in high school because that's just the way our country is. It's all really bad.

There really aren't very many role models anymore. I think the most important role model for someone is their parents, and I know there are tons of kids who live in foster homes, or nowhere, who don't have any parents to look up to. If you don't have someone to guide you and tell you what's right and wrong, then how are you going to find out? You're going to find out on the streets, or from your friends in school who are in the same situation as you are.

If your parents aren't serious, if you're doing bad in school and the teacher calls your parents and they don't do anything, they don't care, why should you care? You're a kid. You don't know what to do.

We need to reevaluate what we feel is important in society. Right now violence is a very important thing in our society. For some reason, everyone loves it. People go to the movies to see people get shot and killed. They like to see blood. That's what sells. Violence and sex and all that stuff. It sells. If that's the way our society is going to continue to go, we're just not going to make it.

AMY: Every time I'd interview someone, I'd ask, Who's your role model, who do you look up to? And usually they'd say, My big brother, he's in a gang, he beats up people every day. And I was like, Don't you look up to your parents? And they'd say stuff like, My mom sleeps all day or my dad sells drugs. I just can't imagine not having *any*one to look up to who's a positive influence in your life.

TJ: I think that's why gangs are formed, because there's nobody to look up to. Gangs are a substitute when families aren't there. If there could be somebody in the community they could go to and look up to, instead of gangs, maybe it could start to change things.

HECTOR: You have to live a positive life, don't always think that everything is going to turn on negative. If you live a negative life, you're never going to get anywhere. How do you expect to become something in life if you're saying, Oh, I'm not going to make it, I'm not going to do this and I'm not going to do that?

CAT: People are having a hard time holding steady jobs. Their parents don't hold steady jobs. They could be living in a welfare hotel next month if they don't scrape by this month. It's like you have no real ties to the society. And if you have nothing keeping you together, you have nothing to lose. I think that's why there's so much violence—you really don't have anything to lose in going to jail. If you don't have an identity or a goal that you're working toward, then what do you have?

SARAH: I think violence relates to poverty because if you don't have any money, you have to steal things so that you can have them. Or you can sell drugs. So we need to help people who are poor, more than we're doing now. I'm really glad we have a new President, because the other two weren't doing anything except making it a lot worse.

Kids shouldn't have to grow up with violence in their homes or on their streets or in their schools or anywhere. It's ridiculous that you need a metal detector to get into school. A school is a place where kids are supposed to learn and then go to the next school. It's not a place for drugs and guns and knives and things like that. It just really angers me that our world has come to this.

HECTOR: I think television is also a big problem. When you see this family, like on "Beverly Hills, 90210," living this good life and all their problems get solved and they have a car and people say, Why should I not have a life like that? I'll do anything to get that way, and that's like another way to promote violence. I'm never going to be like those people, so I'll just push my way through. And if you have this mentality, that you're harder than everyone else, you're definitely not going to do it by education. You're going to do it by force. You're going to fight your way up there, use your hands, kill people, deal drugs.

SARAH: I have hope for a lot of kids in America but not for all. I'm really upset about all the crack babies that are born. When they're born they already have something against them. They're already addicted to a drug. And no one wants them. Their mothers, their fathers, no one wants them. No one wants to adopt babies with AIDS, either.

I don't know what we can do, but every person that wants to help makes it better. I think we have to work together and figure out something to do. Bill Clinton cannot make our country not violent. He's one person. Even his administration is just going to be a bureaucratic organization. What are they going to do? Write laws. But laws obviously haven't gotten us anywhere. It's the law that you can't steal. You can't kill. You can't rape. You can't do all these things. But it doesn't matter. It's against the law to sell drugs, but that doesn't help.

I don't think putting people in jail is the answer to all our problems, either. A lot of the violence is happening inside jails. I think we all need to find out our values again. I'm not saying I want it to be like the fifties with the mom and the dad and the mom stays home all day and bakes cookies and they have a little dog and a picket fence. That's not what I want. I just want everyone to be a little kinder instead of trying to be against everybody else who you don't even know.

I haven't seen violence like these kids in the book have. I've heard it from them, but I haven't lived it and so I still can't see why you need to have fifty friends to walk down the street with you because somebody's going to come and attack you. So now I'm afraid and I think it's a shame that everyone's scared of something. We need to eliminate the fear. If only people could walk down the street and not be afraid they're going to be attacked, that's what I hope for. But I don't know how to do that, either.

Is there anything we can do to make it more hopeful for the youth of America? How can things get better?

SHANE: We need to be a lot more optimistic about it. Although one person can't do a lot, one person *can* do something. One person might inspire someone else to do something. One person can change another person's life, which is a remarkable thing in itself. Just realizing that everyone has the power to do something and if you act on that, instead of sitting back and feeling sad or something, then a lot of stuff can get done.

SARAH: I don't know if I'm that hopeful. There are so many different violences. Even our music is violent. I honestly think that it's in human nature to be violent because we are animals. Animals fight. They kill each other. There's always going to be violence, though when our parents were growing up, society was not at all like this. Then it was mobs and gangs; it was underground and it was seen as bad. Nowadays it looks good when you beat someone else up. That's how you prove to your friends that you are strong and can do anything.

CAT: I don't agree. When our parents were growing up, there were pogroms going on and that's not underground violence. That's very open. That's very open, ethnic violence and that's what's happening today. Like in Bosnia and L.A.

But I don't think it's in human nature, because the only proof of that you can have is if you feel it in yourself, and I don't feel it in myself. Look at the mass *non*violent movements—Gandhi and Martin Luther King. It's when you don't live according to your ideals that things get all messed up. It has to do with living according to what you want to be. I really don't think that most people want to be beaten up. You have to listen to what you know inside to be true.

I think you have to decide for yourself what you want to be and where your life is going to go. No matter how many government programs they make to get people off the street, it's not going to work unless people want to get off the street. There's no institutional solution for violence. It's all to do with the individual and that's why I think you need individual role models, because it's such a personal thing.

You have to have a strong character. If you want to make it through adolescence without getting killed, you're going to have to have a strong character. Like being your own leader. There's no way you're going to build a person's self-esteem and character from a government program.

What I feel inside to be true is that the world can get better and that we don't have to have violence. There's enough horrible things that happen without having to deal with violence. We have so many hardships already in the world, we're placed on the planet with a whole bunch of dangerous things that could happen to us. Why make our problems worse by making guns?

HECTOR: Most of the kids have too much to prove. You go looking for some guy because you want to have a fight, you want to prove to him that you have more people than he does. What's up here is what counts. It's in your mind. I don't think fighting is the answer to anything. But two years ago, that's all I was doing was fighting.

You just have to separate yourself from those who are going to drag you down. That's what it's really about. To separate yourself. I don't mean to be a hermit or anything, just be there and know who your real friends are 'cause some of them are not going to be there for you in the future.

239

SARAH: When I was a little kid, I walked to school by myself. I didn't know it then, but my mom followed behind me to make sure I got there okay. Now, in 1993, I'm a lot older and there's no way that I would walk to school by myself, and I live in one of the most safe neighborhoods in New York. I'm scared of this city now. I don't like it here anymore. I've been taught that to live here, you don't look at anyone in the eye. If you do, you're asking for it. It's just an unwritten rule. It's such a hostile environment. Maybe if people could be a little more friendly, then maybe we wouldn't all be so violent. I don't understand why everyone needs to prove something to everybody else. I just wish we could all get along, but it's not going to happen anytime soon. I don't think so.

RANDY: I tried to talk with the kids we interviewed about how they would end the violence, but they were like, Well, you can't. It didn't encourage me about the future of kids in the United States at all. I'm really worried about them, like what are these kids going to do when they turn eighteen? Are they going to go ahead and join a gang? Are they going to become murderers? I'm more worried than encouraged about the future.

MICHELLE: What three words would you use to describe the future of kids?

RANDY: *Chaos, trials,* and *tribulations.*

MICHELLE: I would say *struggle.* But also *light,* keep the light in the tunnel so they can get there. *Hope,* maybe. And *dreamers,* you have to be a dreamer, keep in front of you what you want your future to be.

RANDY: Yeah, if you don't have a dream, you don't have a future.

Does whether you turn out to be a violent criminal or a normal, productive member of society, then, just come down to what you have inside yourself?

240

CAT: I think it comes down to what you have inside you, but it's also your circumstances. You have to assert your independence in adolescence, but you also have to have something you can fall back on when you're feeling terrible and awful in adolescence.

The majority of times you're going to turn out better if you have a really healthy, decent background where you feel like you've got support from your family or support from someone else, than if you feel like you're all alone and you've always been all alone through your whole life and you've had to assert your independence since you were two or since you were born. Like crack babies struggling to survive since they come out of the womb—I mean, that's crazy. You can't struggle your whole life and expect to turn out a healthy member of society.

SHANE: I don't think one person I interviewed came from a family that was supportive of them, that listened to what they were saying or cared about their progress. You know, when you're growing up, it's really hard for a seven-year-old to stand up by themselves when they still have to rely on their parents for food and shelter and their parents don't really want to give it. It depends a lot on the character of the person, but it also depends on how much they can stand and how strong they can be against the kind of stuff they have to face. There's only so much a person can stand.

Do you think that the kids you interviewed—the ones who are really in trouble—do you think they'll be able to make it in the future? Do you think they'll be able to change?

ERIC: I think you could make it if you really put yourself to do it. It's true, if they've been hurt or if their life's been going wrong all their life, then it will be hard, but they still have time to change. They don't realize it, but there's a lot of people out there who care about them, and there's a lot of people out there who could help them. If they can just pick up their self-esteem—maybe not all the way up, but pick some of it up—

241

then, if they start to unwind from there, if they can realize that, Damn, somebody does care for me, maybe there's hope. You cannot say that there won't be no hope because that's just putting the person down all the way. I say, whoever's reading this book, keep trying, do your best, all around the world, just keep striving. That's the main thing.

ROLANDO: I say we do have hope. It's never too late. Never say never. To all the young kids out there, just think about what you're doing and do the right thing. Don't mess up. You have a whole life ahead of you. Go to school, get an education. Without a high-school diploma you ain't nobody in the world today.

ERIC: You know, I used to look at drug dealers and say, Damn, they never gonna make it. They look all busted, all crack-headed, but then when I started working on this book, I started relating to people like that—drug dealers, people who committed crimes. And I can see in them that they want to do something about it. They may feel they can't get help, but they could. So I've been wrong all this time saying that they be worthless, that they never gonna make it.

People need to pay more attention to people that are in trouble, that need help. All these people in politics, with money, they don't see that there's a lot of people out there who need help.

ROLANDO: After people take a look at this book and, I hope really read the book, they're going to realize, Wow, there's people out there with problems. They have nobody for them. They need somebody to talk to.

And meanwhile there's people in their houses, big beautiful houses, saying this and that, watching the news, watching all these homeless people and all they're thinking about is, Well, at least I'm not like that. At least I got my money. I don't have to worry about nothing like that.

For the people that's reading this book right now, all I'm

saying is, Don't be selfish in life. Don't think, I've got this and that, so I've got nothing to worry about. Because one day, you never know. All of that could go down the drain and just sweep away and then you might see something was wrong, but by then it may be too late.

How do you think the future will be? Do you think this book will make a difference?

ERIC: I'm real afraid and I just want to say to drug dealers out there, Yo, take it easy. I understand that you want to make your money, maybe because you're not living too good, but you gotta also realize that it's causing a lot of problems, man, it's like taking lives away that are innocent. A couple of buildings down from my building I see kids buying stuff down in the basement, and I say to myself, Damn, these kids are going to end up one day getting shot or behind bars or six feet under. Violence don't stop when there's drug dealing. The whole world's gonna come apart.

I hope this book will help kids who are in trouble. I think this book is a real good hit because it's talking straight up about the problems that we're facing today. This is it, man. I feel like the effect of these kids in this book is gonna be powerful. It's gonna be powerful because they're talking dead-up nineties-style, you know, the real thing. Raw.

ROLANDO: I hope this book will knock some sense into people's heads. Maybe it won't, maybe it will. You never know. I hope they'll think about it, think about it twice. And if they don't pay attention to it . . .

ERIC: Maybe they'll give it to somebody else, another hoodlum.

I'm glad I got into Children's Express 'cause I got to travel, learn about more things, learn about other people's lives, meet new people. I'm still that type of hoodlum that I was, I'll never change that style. But I have changed a lot inside. People still look at me as a hoodlum but, you know, there's more than just looking at a person like that. I know I really look like a hoodlum, but deep down inside, you meet me, and I'm a real nice person.

ROLANDO: When I see violence on the streets, I try to avoid it. But sometimes violence comes to me because of the way I dress or the way I look. It's always approaching me, but I try to avoid it, I try to walk away from it. I think the violence in this world should change 'cause we ain't getting nowhere. People should realize what they're doing, try to stop it, just let it come to an end. If it doesn't come to an end, it's going to reach a point that one day the world is just going to end 'cause everybody's killing each other.

This book tells you all the facts of life, and I just want to say to all you kids that are out there, if you're reading this and you're a drug dealer, if you think you're all big and bad 'cause you're making money, come on, man. Your mother herself is thinking, Oh, my God, look what my son is doing. Come on, man, that's your mother. She carried you for nine months in her stomach, and you think she wants to see her kid go behind bars for drug dealing? Wake up, man. This is the nineties. Wake up.

ACKNOWLEDGMENTS

Children's Express wishes to gratefully acknowledge the support of the Prudential Foundation, which made this book possible, and Peter Goldberg, the foundation's president, whose vision it was.

This book is the work of many people. Those whose stories were included here spoke from their hearts about their agony and their hope. We are indebted to them for their candor and their willingness to tell their stories to virtual strangers. The Children's Express teenage editors who traveled across the country to conduct the interviews infused their work with energy, enthusiasm, and remarkable insight. Project Director Nick Terranova and Indianapolis Children's Express Bureau Director Lynn Sygiel guided their work with creativity, tenderness, and skill.

The editors' several hundred interviews were lovingly transcribed by Mary Spohn and Ada Parkinson in Indianapolis and Joyce Hellew and Keisha Settle in New York. Their work was otherwise enabled and encouraged by Cliff Hahn, Dina Hirsch, Mia McDonald, Charlotte Savidge, Suzanne Preston, Madelyn Morgan, Charlie Lord, and Lee Wood in the Children's Express bureaus in New York, Indianapolis, and Washington.

Among the many people across the country who welcomed and assisted our editors, we especially thank:

Dr. Jacqueline Brown at the Atlanta Children's Shelter and Erica Carson at Exodus in Atlanta, Georgia.

Sue Vashti at the Pacific Center for Human Growth in Berkeley, California.

Cheryl Orr at Girls Inc., Ralph Done at Boys Club, Nancy Bellinger and Susan Whitten at the YMCA, Damon Ellison at the Juvenile Detention Center, the Woodruff Place Baptist Church, Carol Morris at Big Sisters, Damon Broadbecker, Paul Pycett, Dave Uberto, Chris Malloy, and Pamela Klein at Boys School/Girls School at Plainfield, Tawanna Clarke at the Girl Scouts, Dave Wagner at the Carver Community Organization, Judith Meyers-Walls at Purdue University, and Joan Schneider in Indianapolis.

Reverend Chang Soon Lee at the Wilshire United Methodist Church, Pastor Cecil Murray at the First AME Church, Gloria Newell at the Los Angeles County Office of Education, Roger Tobey and Willie Fobbs of the Metropolitan Specialized Gang Unit, and Allen Wouse in Los Angeles, California.

District Attorney Kathy Baker in Miami, Oklahoma.

Bonnie Berkowitz at the Children's Aid Society, Susan Montez at FACES, and our friends at the Resolving Conflict Creatively program and Alateen in New York City.

Leota Rousch and Pat Parillo at St. Luke's Church, Diana Rangel at the Youth Drop-In Center, Catherine Causay at St. Patrick's Church, Howard Curry at Teens Court, Sgt. Ruben Gonzalez and Troy Smith at PAL, Susan McAuliffe at San Antonio Light, and Nathaniel and Rudy at the YMCA in San Antonio, Texas.

Dionne Monning at the Larkin South Youth Center in San Francisco, California.

Ray McClasland at the Boys Club in San Jose, California.

Richard Gordon at Community Youth Services in San Mateo, California.

Jay Vaughn and Daniel P. Altman at the National Crime Prevention Council, Sergeant Williams, Officer Bullock, and Sergeant Langley of the Police Department, Joe Williams and Brian Smith of the I Have a Dream Foundation, and Becki Ali at Sasha Bruce Youth Works in Washington, D.C.

246

We also give special thanks to Manny in New York, Refugio in San Francisco, Melissa in Atlanta, and Roger in Los Angeles, who were our guides to the underground life of teens living in the streets of their cities. They helped CE editors gain access to and acceptance among kids in gangs. They introduced us to young people who otherwise might not have talked to us.

I am indebted to and thank David Nee, Executive Director of the Ittleson Foundation, who served as mentor and guide through new territory, to Page Ashley, Children's Express Board member and editorial impressario extraordinaire, and to Bob Clampitt, founder, president, and beloved guiding spirit of Children's Express, who ignited my interest and kept alive my faith that we really could produce a book from the thousands of pages of raw material exuberantly produced by CE's editors.

Others to whom I am deeply grateful for their counsel and critiques are: Mary Goodwillie, Perdita Huston, Harry Mattison, Wendy Puriefoy, Susan Reichman, Bruce Stedman, and Phyllis Wender. I appreciate and thank Holly Morris and Sean Foley for their patient lifting of my computer literacy to new heights.

All of us are grateful to and thank Betty Prashker, editor-in-chief at the Crown Publishing Group, for believing in our idea in the first place and, with Kim Reilly's able assistance, for guiding our creative process with patience and wit.

—S.G.

ABOUT THE CHILDREN'S
EXPRESS EDITORS

CHANDA BOYDEN

Chanda is a sophomore at Tri West High School in Lizton, Indiana. She is editor of her school newspaper, on the Student Council, and a member of Students Against Drunk Driving (SADD). She wants to be a journalist when she graduates from college. She got involved with Children's Express because she loves to meet all kinds of new people and talk to them about things that they do, whether they're famous or in the fifth grade.

SUKI CHEONG

Suki was born in Singapore and later moved to New York City. She now lives in Washington Heights and has been a reporter and editor for Children's Express' New York bureau for five years.

ERIN COX

Erin is an energetic high-school junior in Indiana who loves volleyball and singing in the church choir. She hopes that who-ever reads this book will understand and realize that these kids' problems are our problems, too. Her interview with Leigh Ann in an Oklahoma jail helped her to see "that the world isn't TV reality, and certainly isn't perfect."

HECTOR CRUZADO

Hector lives in Yonkers, New York, with his father. He is Puerto Rican, Dominican, and American. He's a sophomore in high school and he loves to dance. Last summer he got beat up and was hospitalized, an experience that made him decide "not to challenge people anymore." He wants to go to college and become a movie director. He is writing a screenplay about "people that kill other people for writing graffiti or for being one person's friend."

CAT DEAKINS

Cat was born in New York City and has lived in Greenwich Village all her life. She's a junior at Stuyvesant High School in Manhattan. She has been a reporter and editor with Children's Express since she was eight years old.

TJ EBEL

TJ came to the United States from her native Germany when she was eleven years old. She is a senior at the Indiana Academy for Science, Mathematics and Humanities and plans to attend the University of Washington in Seattle. She hopes to major in biochemistry with a minor in zoology. In the future she wants to live "out in nowhere by the woods." She thinks that's what a lot of people need, "that piece of nature that maybe would take the edge off of violence." Her dream is to study animals in the wild, especially big cats and whales.

MICHELLE EVANS

Michelle lives in Indianapolis with her father, is a freshman at Howard University, and a reporter for the student newspaper, *The Hilltop*. In high school, she was the opinion editor of the school newspaper and a member of the National Honor Society. "I enjoy writing stories, but I write poetry mostly because it's quicker than writing a whole story." Her dream is to own her own magazine geared toward black teenage girls.

KATHLEEN HUSTAD

Kathleen is a freshman at Indiana University, majoring in journalism, political science, and Spanish. She writes for the *Indiana Daily Student*. In high school, she was founder and president of an environmental club, in Quill and Scroll Society, on student council, and a member of the National Honor Society. Covering the 1992 Democratic National Convention as a Children's Express editor changed her mind about her future. "Before that I wanted to be an MTV deejay, but afterwards I wanted to be a White House correspondent and a war correspondent."

ROLANDO LIRIANO

Rolando attends Sheepshead Bay High School in Brooklyn, New York. He is half Puerto Rican and half Dominican and lives with both his parents. The greatest thing that ever happened to him was traveling to Atlanta and Los Angeles to do the interviews for this book. His dream is to become a basketball star, or possibly a lawyer or an engineer.

RANDY MCDADE

Randy describes himself as a normal teenager, though he "honestly doesn't know what a normal teenager is." His dream is to become a network news journalist and to be actively involved in helping children. "It's so hard for a child to be heard in today's society . . . please listen to us and we'll be able to tell you what's going to happen. We hold the future in our hands."

ROBIN POTASNIK

Robin is now a junior at Carmel High School outside of Indianapolis. She is assistant editor of the school yearbook and likes to read, go sailing, and listen to music by artists like REM and

Simon & Garfunkel. In the future, she wants to major in business or economics. Her experience at Children's Express has "taught me so much more than I ever thought I could learn. It wakes you up to the real problems of the world."

WENDY POTASNIK

Wendy is now a sophomore at the University of Indiana, where she is majoring in journalism with a second concentration in Spanish. She's been interested in writing since the third grade. Shocked by all that she learned about violence in her interviews for this book, she feels she grew as a writer. "To be a writer you have to live life. You have to experience things, get out there and play the game. That's what we did in this project."

ADAM REICHMAN

Adam is a senior at Walt Whitman High School in Bethesda, Maryland. He lives in Washington, D.C., and "would like to see this city set an example for love and peace, not crime." He hopes to see in his lifetime children growing up without being afraid.

KATE SCHNIPPEL

Kate is a senior at Ben Davis High School in Indiana and plans on majoring in chemistry in college so she can be a research scientist. She wants to minor in Islamic studies or Arabic. Kate competes in speech, plays clarinet in the school band, is a passionate runner, and works part-time as a burger server at Wendy's and as a lab technician. Two years ago a friend was playing with a gun and accidentally shot her through the legs. Though scarred, she recovered. "Luckily, it only affected one track season."

JESS SCHEER

Jess is a junior at Grady High School in Atlanta, Georgia, where he is preparing for a career in journalism and is a

member of the National Honor Society. He has ~
chor and producer of Grady News Network and a staff wril
and news editor of his school newspaper, *The Southerner.* Jess
is a policy debater on the varsity circuit and was awarded Outstanding Delegate recognition at Model UN. In 1990, Jess
served as a Friendship Force ambassador to Tbilisi, where he
lived with a family for two weeks just before the Republic of
Georgia declared its independence from the former Soviet
Union.

SHANE TILSTON

Shane was born in Essex, England, and grew up with his mother
in New York, Houston, and East Africa. He is a freshman at
Tufts University, will probably major in English, and loves the
theater and basketball. He hopes this book will encourage people to listen more and try to understand others' points of view
so that change can happen.

AMY WEISENBACH

Amy is a junior in high school in Indiana and plans to study
broadcast journalism in college because she likes to write and
perform. She's a cheerleader and in All State Chorus. As a
summer intern at a local TV station she wrote scripts and
helped with a kids' road show. She credits Children's Express
for teaching her to really listen and take a stand on issues.

SARAH YOUNG

Sarah is an only child, "a lively and determined redhead," who
grew up with her mother in New York City. She attended the
Bronx High School of Science, "where I learned a lot more of
science than I ever wanted to learn," and is now a freshman at
Northwestern University. She wants to be a professional journalist and make a difference in the lives of others through her
journalistic work.

Eric was born in the Dominican Republic and came to the United States when he was five years old. He is a senior at FDR High School in Brooklyn, New York. He hopes to go to the University of Southern California and major in drama. He's a member of FACES, a teenage improvisational theater group, and likes rapping and drawing. "I do graffiti, but not on a wall, on a piece of paper. I think it's nonsense to mess up your own city or community."